AF616646

MARTIN W. KANE

WORKS:

PHOTOGRAPHS OF ENTERPRISE

HAGLEY MUSEUM AND LIBRARY

DISTRIBUTED BY: THE UNIVERSITY OF PENNSYLVANIA PRESS

Published on the occasion of an exhibition at the Hagley Museum and Library, May 2, 1992 - December 30, 1992.

Photography: Martin W. Kane
Historical Photographs and Images reproduced by: Charles A. Foote
Essays: Christopher T. Baer
Design: Michael Gunselman Incorporated
Printing: Garamond Pridemark Press, Inc.
Baltimore, Maryland
Editor: Jill MacKenzie

Funding for this project was provided, in part, by The Lukens Foundation and Wawa, Inc.

Hagley Museum and Library
P.O. Box 3630
Wilmington, Delaware 19807

Distributed by:
The University of Pennsylvania Press
418 Service Drive
Philadelphia, Pennsylvania 19104-6097

Library of Congress
Card Catalog Number 91-78297
Hagley Museum and Library

ISBN 0-8122-1394-7
(University of Pennsylvania Press)

ISBN 0-914650-29-7
(Hagley Museum and Library)

INTRODUCTION

During the heyday of industrial photography large companies often maintained complete photographic departments. Smaller firms relied on employees who were skilled amateurs or on local professional photographers. With some significant exceptions, most of the images produced were meant to serve corporate needs rather than artistic expression. Yet in examining the large collections of industrial photography preserved at institutions such as the Hagley Museum and Library, the Historical Society of Pennsylvania, and the Railroad Museum of Pennsylvania, it is obvious that many of these now-anonymous photographers knew their craft well and often made photographs of exceptional beauty.

Regrettably, the carefully maintained corporate photographic archive and staff photographer have become endangered species. Thus, when given the opportunity by the Hagley Museum and Library to document current business and industrial conditions, I approached the work with the idea of recapturing the spirit of this earlier school of industrial photography. It is out of this project that *Works: Photographs of Enterprise* has evolved.

The enterprises chosen span the spectrum of regional industry but fall far short of defining it. They were selected for what their histories tell us about change and continuity in the workplace.

Works is a celebration of people, productivity, and the environment where work takes place. I am grateful to the organizations that I have photographed for giving me a free hand in choosing the subjects to document. I did not attempt to produce "pretty pictures," nor did I seek out ugly or depressing situations. I have attempted to present a balanced cross section of the organizations and have approached the people photographed with an eye toward maintaining their dignity. I have sought to treat the workers with the same sense of importance as the CEOs.

Works is a work of history. Though these photographs were made between July 1990 and September 1991, the events pictured must be considered documentation of the recent past. The organizations and people continue to change. The photographs in *Works* are images of the ordinary—no accidents, strikes, or Presidential visits—but everyday situations. Unusual events are documented in many other places. In this body of photographs I have tried to capture honestly the commonplace non-events.

I hope that these photographs present a theme that all work is important. We all can be replaced, but in a very real way what we do, our work, cannot be completely replaced. The work done by the women and men on the shop floor is as important as the decisions of the executive. The livelihood of one would not continue without the labors of the other. The organizations I have put on display here do not exist without employees. Baldwin Locomotive is as extinct as any dinosaur. The buildings where the machines once were made remain, the people that made the engines are gone. If we were to remove the workers from the photographs at Boeing Helicopters the images of Baldwin and Boeing would be the same.

— Martin W. Kane

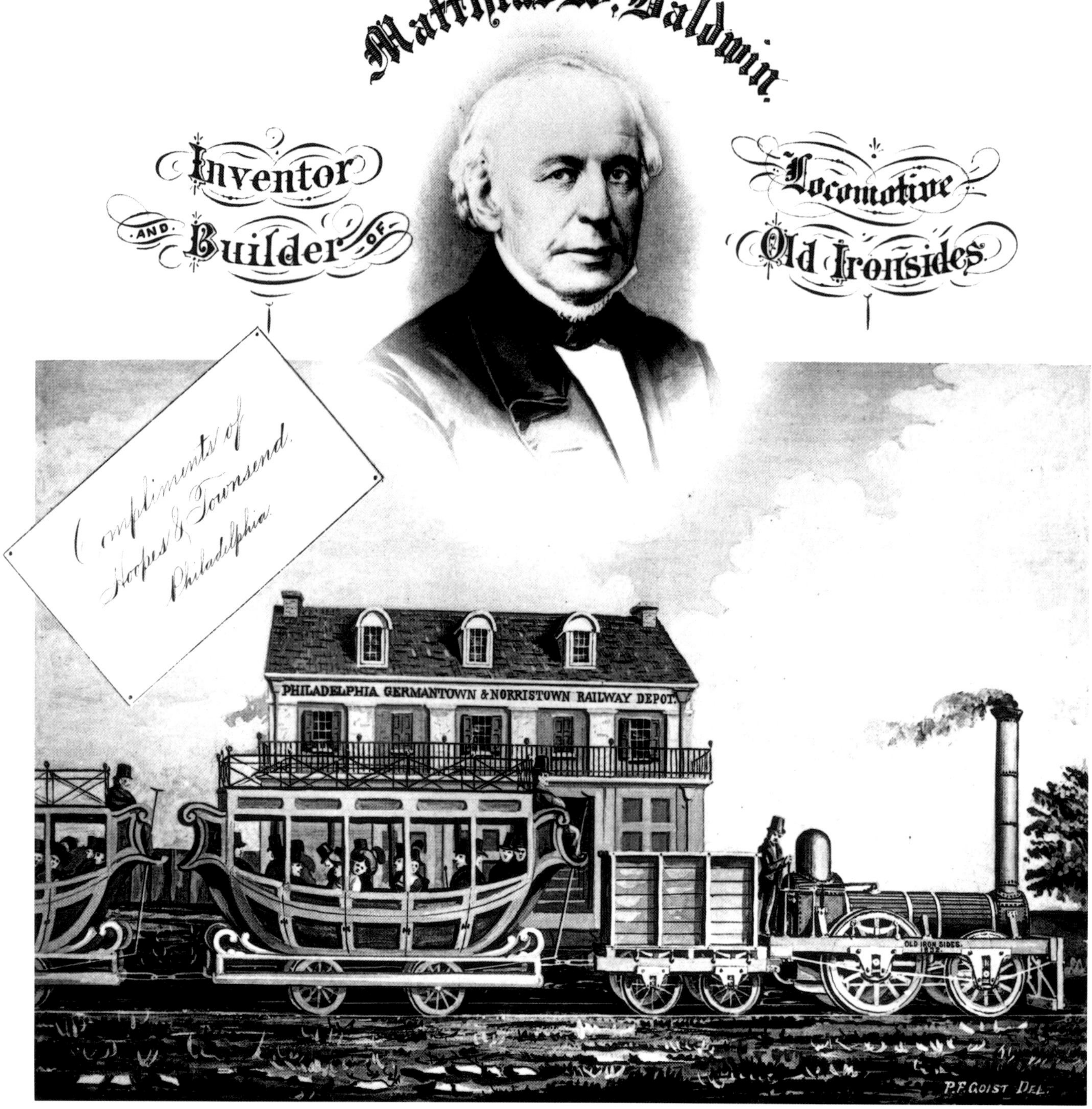

Matthias W. Baldwin

Inventor and Builder of Locomotive Old Ironsides

Compliments of
Hoopes & Townsend
Philadelphia

PHILADELPHIA GERMANTOWN & NORRISTOWN RAILWAY DEPOT.

OLD IRON SIDES

P.F. GOIST DEL.

MACHINERY IN MOTION:

FROM BALDWIN LOCOMOTIVES TO BOEING HELICOPTERS

MATTHIAS WILLIAM BALDWIN (1795-1866), FOUNDER OF THE BALDWIN LOCOMOTIVE WORKS, AND HIS FIRST LOCOMOTIVE, THE OLD IRONSIDES, SHOWN ON ITS FIRST TRIP IN 1832. TAKEN FROM AN 1883 ADVERTISEMENT.

M. W. BALDWIN & Co. PHILa.
Plan C.

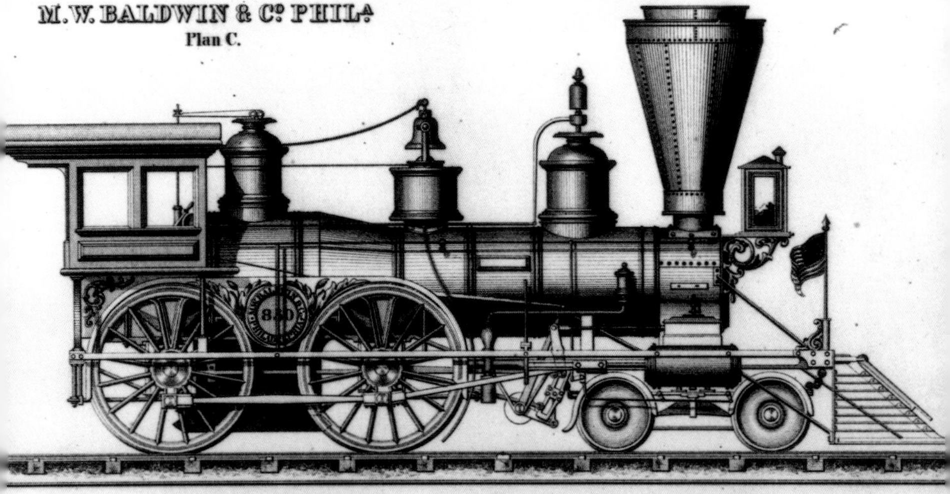

850

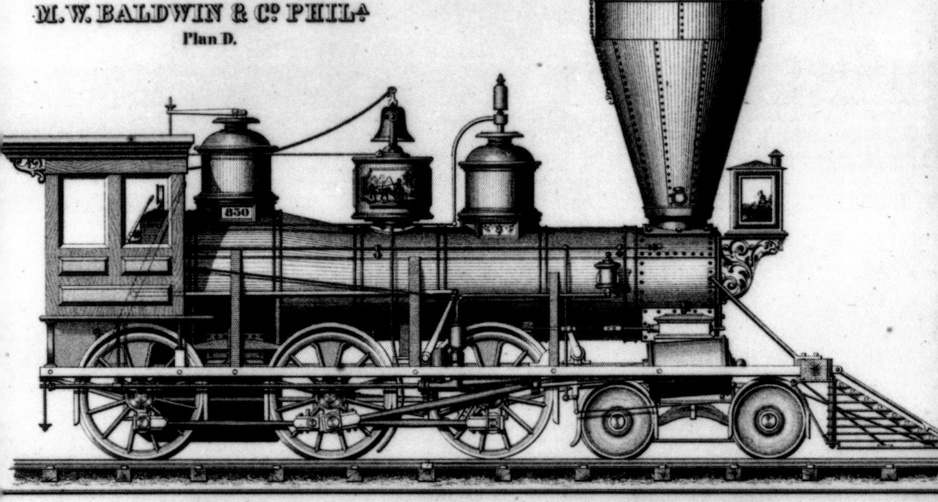

M. W. BALDWIN & Co. PHILa.
Plan D.

M. W. BALDWIN & Co. PHILa.
Plan E.

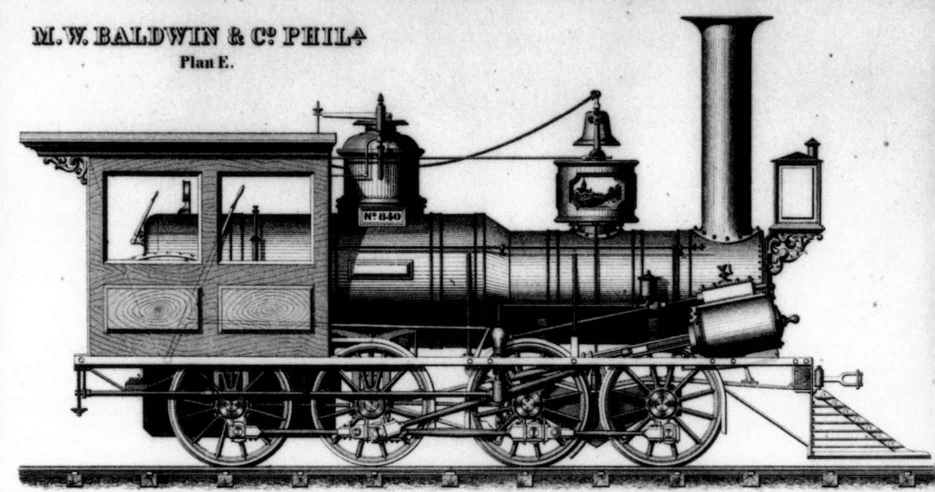

No firm so epitomized Philadelphia's role as a manufacturing center as the Baldwin Locomotive Works, packed into twenty acres just north of the heart of the city. It was for a time the largest locomotive builder in the world, whose products could be found in practically every country where there were railroads.

Matthias W. Baldwin was born in Elizabeth, New Jersey in 1795, and was apprenticed to a Philadelphia jeweler at sixteen. In 1825 he formed a partnership with David Mason, a machinist and wood engraver. In 1827 Baldwin built a six-horsepower stationary steam engine, now in the Smithsonian Institution, to power his shop. Within three years he was on his own as an engine-builder. In 1831 he produced a working model locomotive for Charles Wilson Peale's museum that was capable of pulling four passengers around a circular track. This led to an order from a new local railroad, the Philadelphia, Germantown & Norristown. After further experience gained in helping assemble an imported Stephenson locomotive at New Castle, Delaware, Baldwin produced the *Old Ironsides,* essentially a copy of the English model. *Old Ironsides* made its first trip on November 23, 1832, to much public acclaim. At the time the *Philadelphia Chronicle* wrote, "We rejoice at the result of this experiment, as it conclusively shows that Philadelphia, always famous for the skill of her mechanics, is enabled to produce a steam engine for railroads combining so many superior qualities as to warrant the belief that her mechanics will hereafter supply nearly all the public works of this description in the country."

In 1835 Baldwin built a three-story factory at Broad and Hamilton Streets, which became the core of the future works. Baldwin was a very conservative builder who was late to adopt innovations. His locomotives were simple, cheap, and reliable. He also came to realize the necessity of teamwork. The recurring panics and depressions of the 1830s, 1840s, and 1850s forced Baldwin to search out financial support wherever it might be found, and this accounts for his survival, while most of the other Philadelphia locomotive builders failed. A succession of partners also provided the financial and managerial skills that Baldwin himself lacked. His company became an organization that easily survived the death of its founder in 1866.

The Baldwin Locomotive Works remained a self-renewing partnership and did not become a public company until 1911. By 1873 it was the nation's largest locomotive builder, producing more than 400 locomotives a year and employing almost 3,000 men and boys.

After a forty-year period of relative stability, American locomotive design underwent rapid evolutionary change between the late 1890s and World War I. These were Baldwin's golden years, when it commanded 40 percent of the American locomotive market. The company systematized the production of locomotives using a labor system of subcontractors and piece-work. Subassemblies produced in this fashion by dozens of specialized trades were brought together in the bays of the erecting shop and assembled into a finished locomotive. Baldwin built to customer specifications, since steam locomotives had to meet particular local service conditions and burn the cheapest locally-available fuel. While there was a great deal of standardization, and the largest railroads generally placed orders for large lots, Baldwin was proud of its ability to build whatever the customer

BALDWIN STANDARD PRODUCTS OF THE CIVIL WAR ERA FOLLOWED THE CLASSIFICATION SYSTEM DEVELOPED BY ONE-TIME PARTNER ASA WHITNEY. PLAN "C" WAS THE 4-4-0 AMERICAN TYPE, THE STANDARD, ALL PURPOSE LOCOMOTIVE FROM THE 1840S THROUGH THE 1880S.

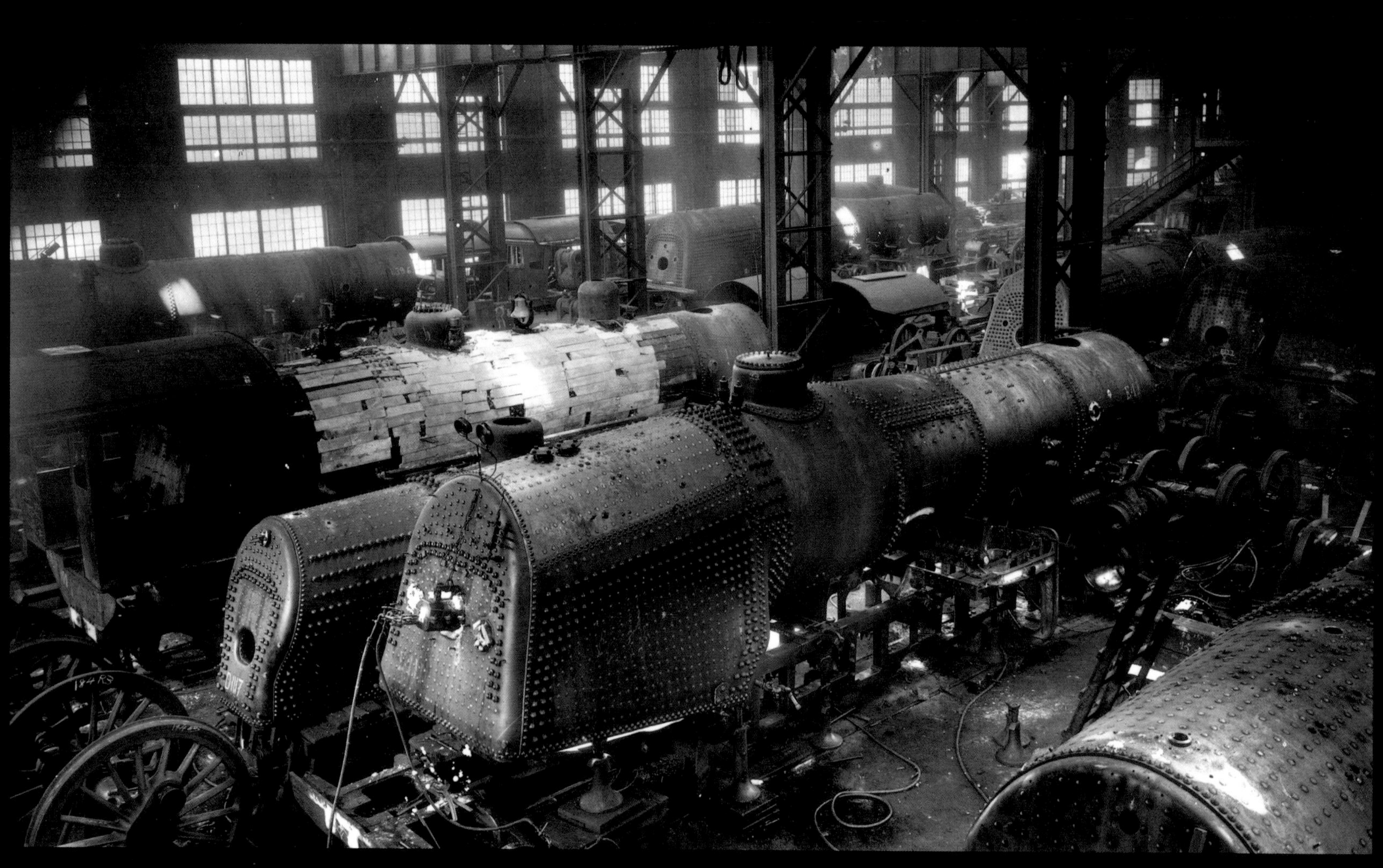

wanted, no matter how unorthodox, and it was able to market locomotives in most European countries and around the world. Most of its domestic competitors were forced to merge into the American Locomotive Company (ALCO) in 1901 in order to match Baldwin's economies of scale.

Larger locomotives could not be built within the cramped confines of the old shops in Philadelphia so the firm began buying land in 1906, eventually exceeding 600 acres, at Eddystone on the Delaware River south of the city. Production was gradually shifted, until the last part of the Philadelphia Works was closed in 1928. Everything about Eddystone was superlative. Unfortunately, it had been designed on the assumptions of 1905 and the boom years of World War I. Baldwin peaked in 1923, well before Eddystone was completed. In that year the company grossed more than $100 million and employed 21,500 workers. By 1928, the year Eddystone was dedicated with pride and pageantry, the gross had fallen to $22.5 million and the work force to 7,500.

Railroads were already losing their near-monopoly of ground transportation, and in response, the steam locomotive was entering the final stage of its development: larger, faster, and more powerful than it had ever been. The first advances in "super power" came not from tradition-minded Baldwin, but from the upstart Lima Locomotive Works in Ohio, which until 1915 had built mostly specialized logging locomotives. Baldwin copied the "super power" concept, but faster, more powerful locomotives also meant that fewer locomotives were needed. Now locomotive frames were cast as a single piece of steel with integral cylinders, where previously they had to be fabricated from as many as 800 separate pieces. Jobs vanished by the thousands. Then came the Depression, drying up orders. The company diversified into heavy machinery, trying to keep Eddystone alive. Then came the diesel.

Contrary to popular conception, Baldwin was not wedded to steam. It had been building electric locomotives in partnership with Westinghouse since the beginnings of mainline electric traction in the mid-1890s. It built its first diesel in 1925, just after the first commercial diesel went on the market, but Baldwin was late in developing road units and fell afoul of a new competitor, General Motors. GM built diesels like it built cars: a few standard models, a few options, your choice of color. It produced a road passenger unit in 1935 and a freight unit in 1939.

World War II saw a large portion of Eddystone devoted to military production. Only GM was allowed to build road diesels, giving it a four-year lead. Baldwin introduced its own line of road locomotives in 1945, but it built them like steam engines, to customer specifications. Baldwin never secured more than 13 percent of the diesel market, well behind GM and ALCO. It also built several costly and unsuccessful steam turbine locomotives in a last-ditch attempt to prevent the demise of steam. Lima's venture in to the diesel market was even less successful, and on December 4, 1950, it merged with Baldwin to form the Baldwin-Lima-Hamilton Corporation. The last Baldwin locomotive, a diminutive switcher, left Eddystone in 1956.

In the early 1960s a small portion of the Eddystone plant was purchased by Boeing Vertol and transformed into a helicopter manufacturing facility. Like Baldwin, Vertol owed its existence to a single entrepreneur, Frank N. Piasecki, an early helicopter

LOCOMOTIVES UNDER CONSTRUCTION IN THE EDDYSTONE SECTION "A" ERECTING SHOP IN 1913. THE SHOP COVERED SEVEN AND ONE HALF ACRES AND HAD A CAPACITY OF FIFTY LARGE LOCOMOTIVES PER WEEK. (RAILROAD MUSEUM OF PENNSYLVANIA)

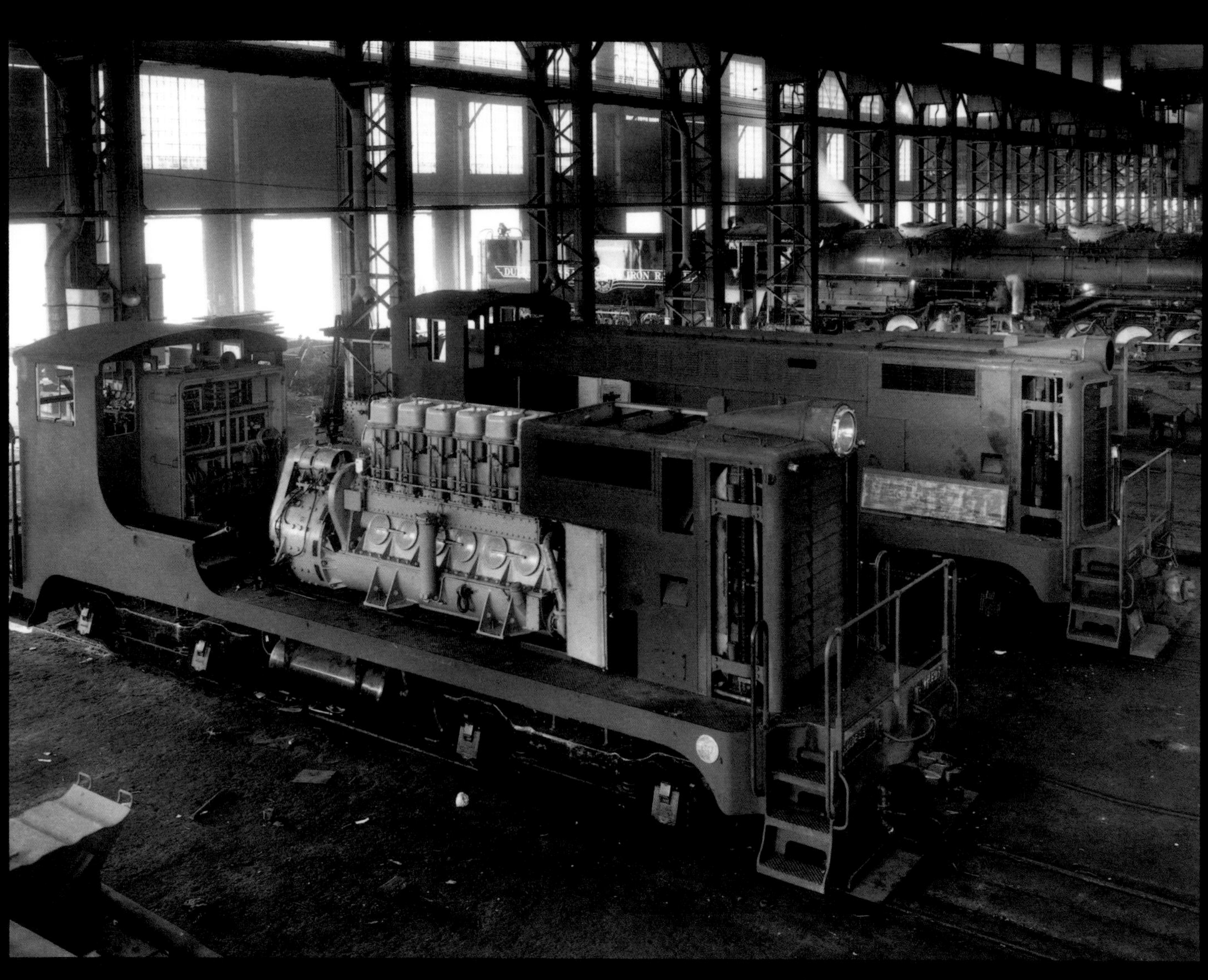

enthusiast, who formed a small company with some fellow Penn engineering students in 1940. The group produced a small prototype in 1943. Unlike Baldwin, Piasecki was a genuine innovator, who pioneered the twin-rotor helicopter. With dual lift, payloads need not be carefully balanced, as with single-rotor choppers. This makes it ideal for transport service, particularly in combat. Piasecki secured his first Navy contract in 1944.

Also unlike Baldwin, Piasecki could not harmonize his greater inventive genius with the demands of his financial backers. They parted company in 1955, Piasecki to continue his experimental work, the others to refine the proven models that Piasecki had already produced under the name of the Vertol Aircraft Corporation. In 1960 they sold the company to Boeing. Perhaps its most famous product was the CH-47 Chinook, first produced in 1961 and used extensively during the Vietnam War. Currently, the early Chinooks are being completely rebuilt and upgraded. The company, now simply known as Boeing Helicopters, is also developing and testing the V-22 Osprey tiltrotor aircraft.

Superficially, Boeing's helicopters and Baldwin's steam behemoths may seem as different as birds and brontosaurs, yet the two are related species. Like locomotives, helicopters are too big to be built on a moving assembly line and are erected in bays by bringing together a number of specialized subassemblies. Metal is pressed, shaped, riveted, and sandblasted, but now everything is thin and light for maximum strength and minimum weight. Instead of heavy pipes and valves, the controls are electronic. The progression toward greater efficiency, lighter construction, conservation of materials, and precision of performance and control that was seen in the steam-to-diesel transition, here finds its latest expression.

THE PAST AND FUTURE MET IN EDDYSTONE ERECTING SHOP IN 1941. IN THE FOREGROUND ARE TWO 660-HORSEPOWER DIESEL SWITCHERS; BEHIND IS A CLASS M-3 LOCOMOTIVE FOR THE DULUTH, MISSABE & IRON RANGE, ONE OF BALDWIN'S LARGEST AND MOST POWERFUL STEAM ENGINES. (RAILROAD MUSEUM OF PENNSYLVANIA)

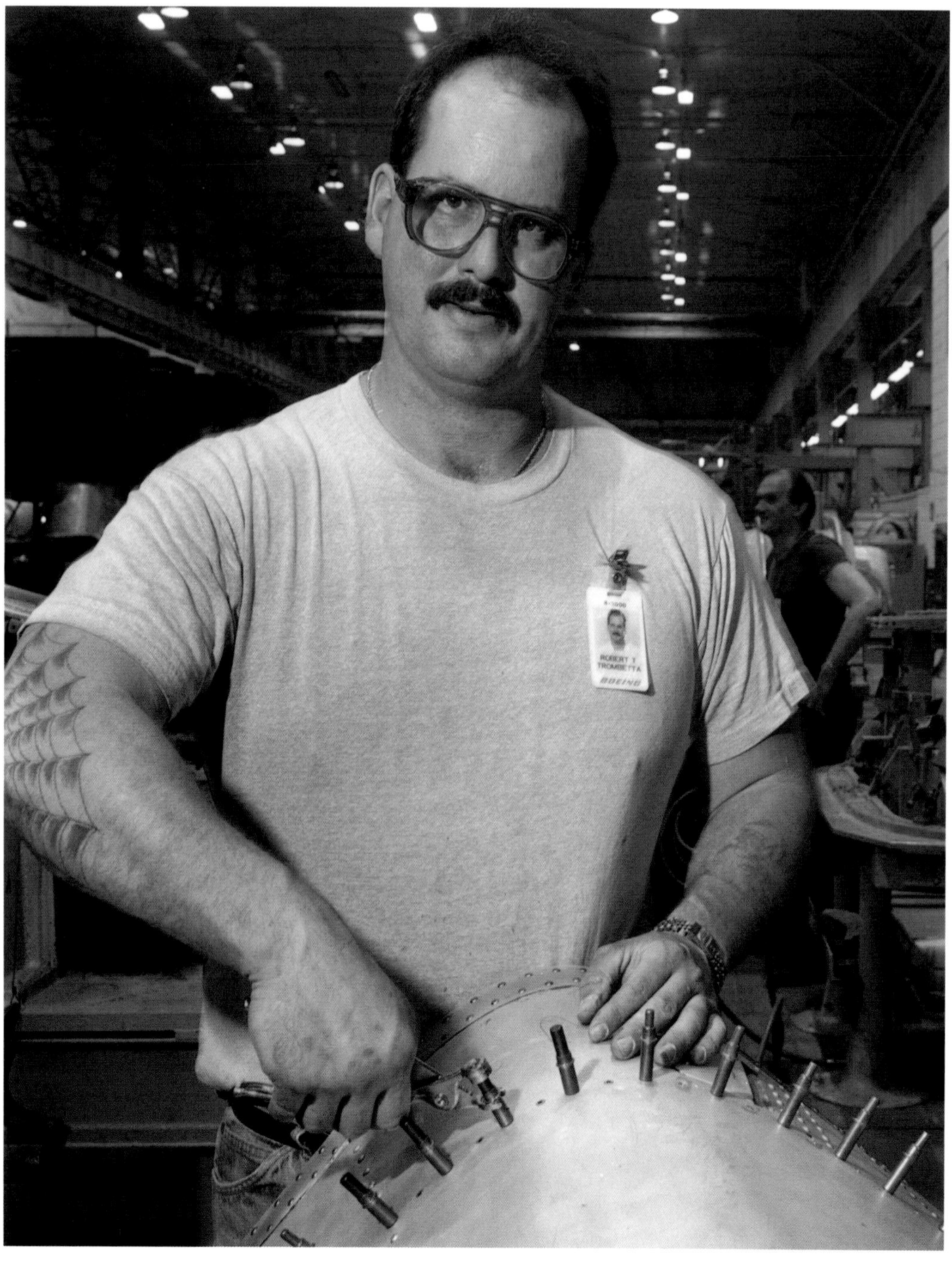

ROBERT TROMBETTA ASSEMBLES A COWLING IN THE "POTS AND PANS SHOP" AT BOEING HELICOPTERS.

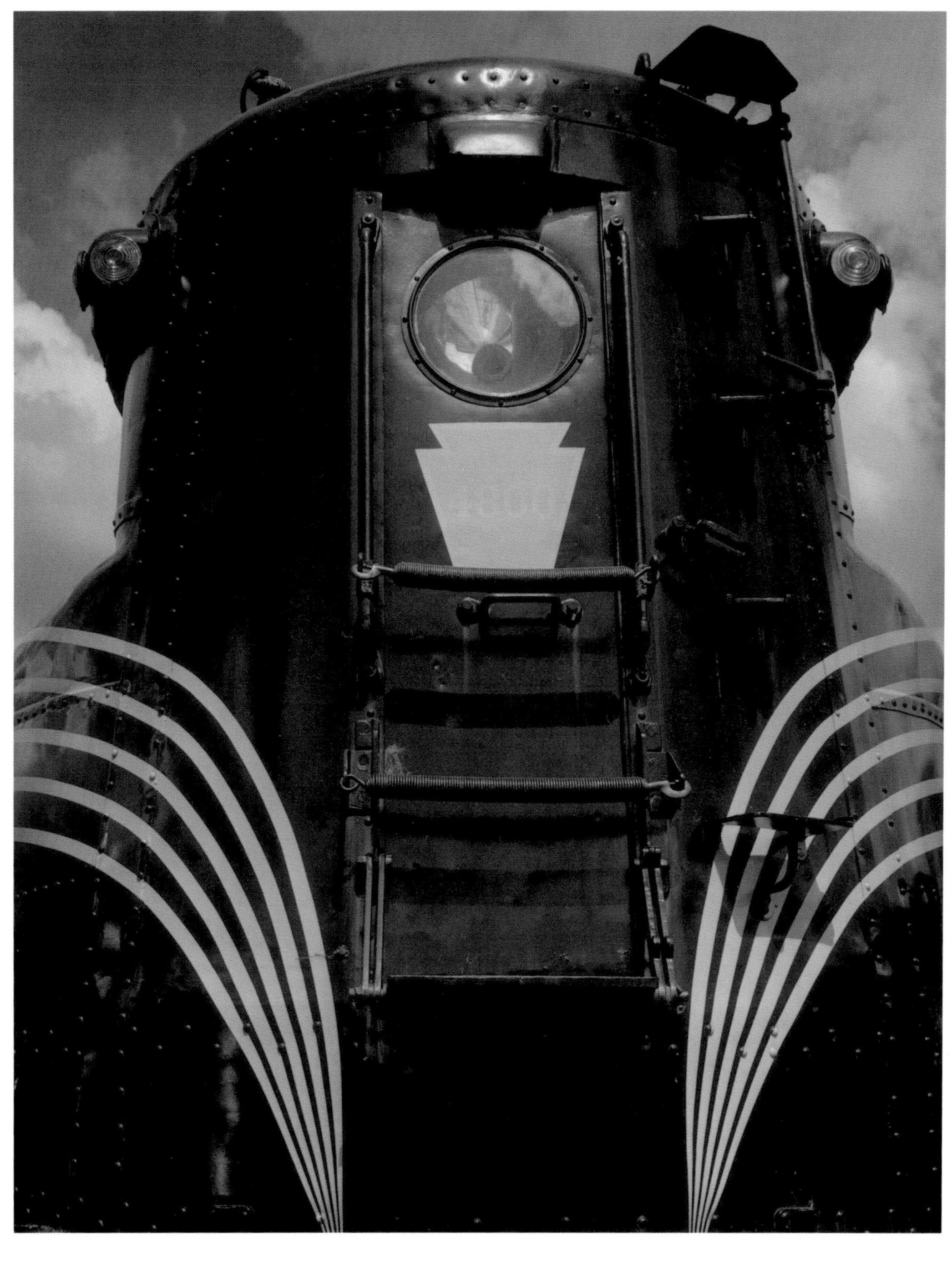

"OLD RIVETS," THE PROTOTYPE PENNSYLVANIA RAILROAD GG-1 ELECTRIC LOCOMOTIVE.

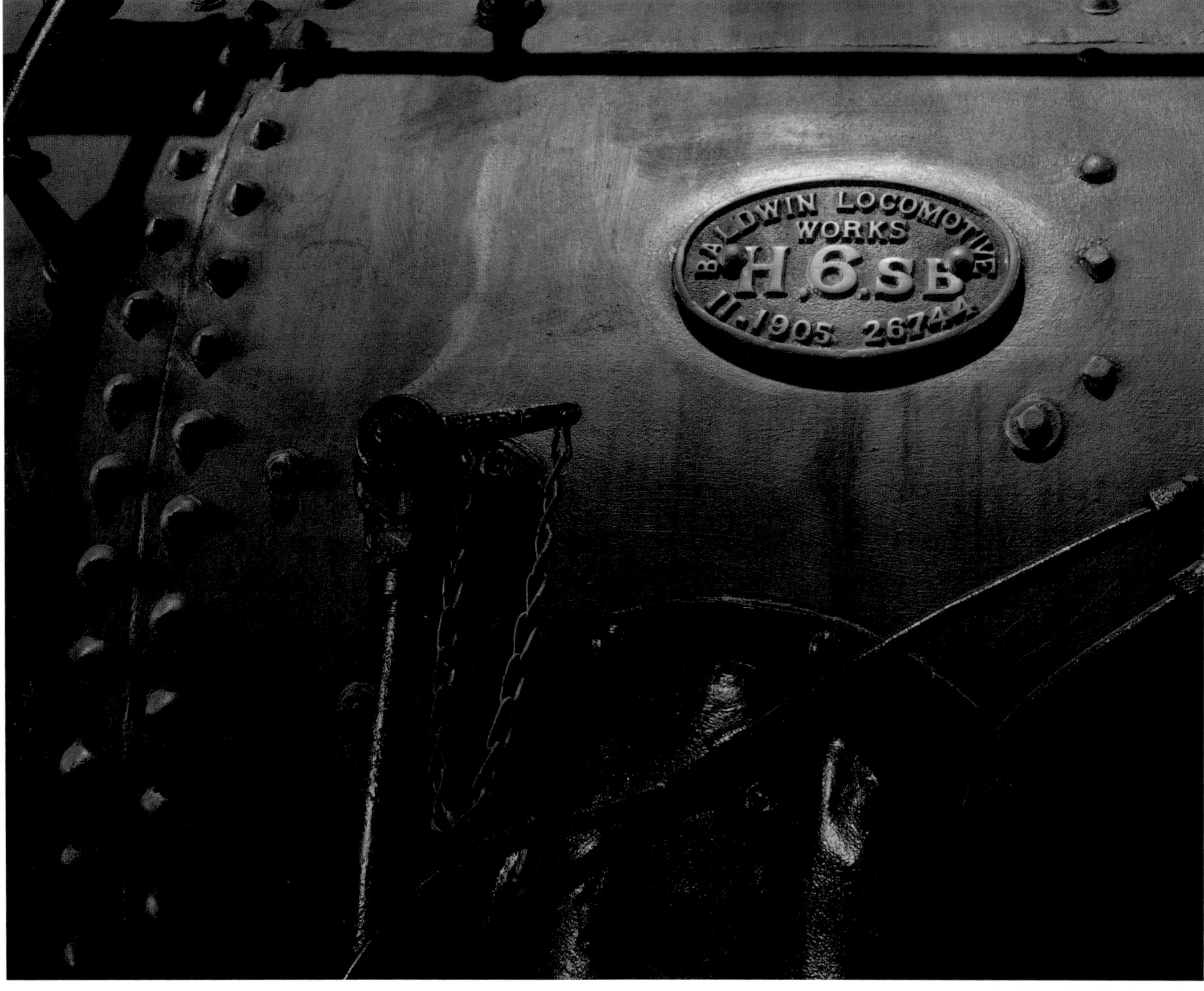

THE CIRCULAR BALDWIN BUILDER'S PLATE WAS KNOWN WORLD-WIDE.

RIGHT: TWO BOEING CH-47D CHINOOK HELICOPTERS AT DIFFERENT STAGES OF COMPLETION.

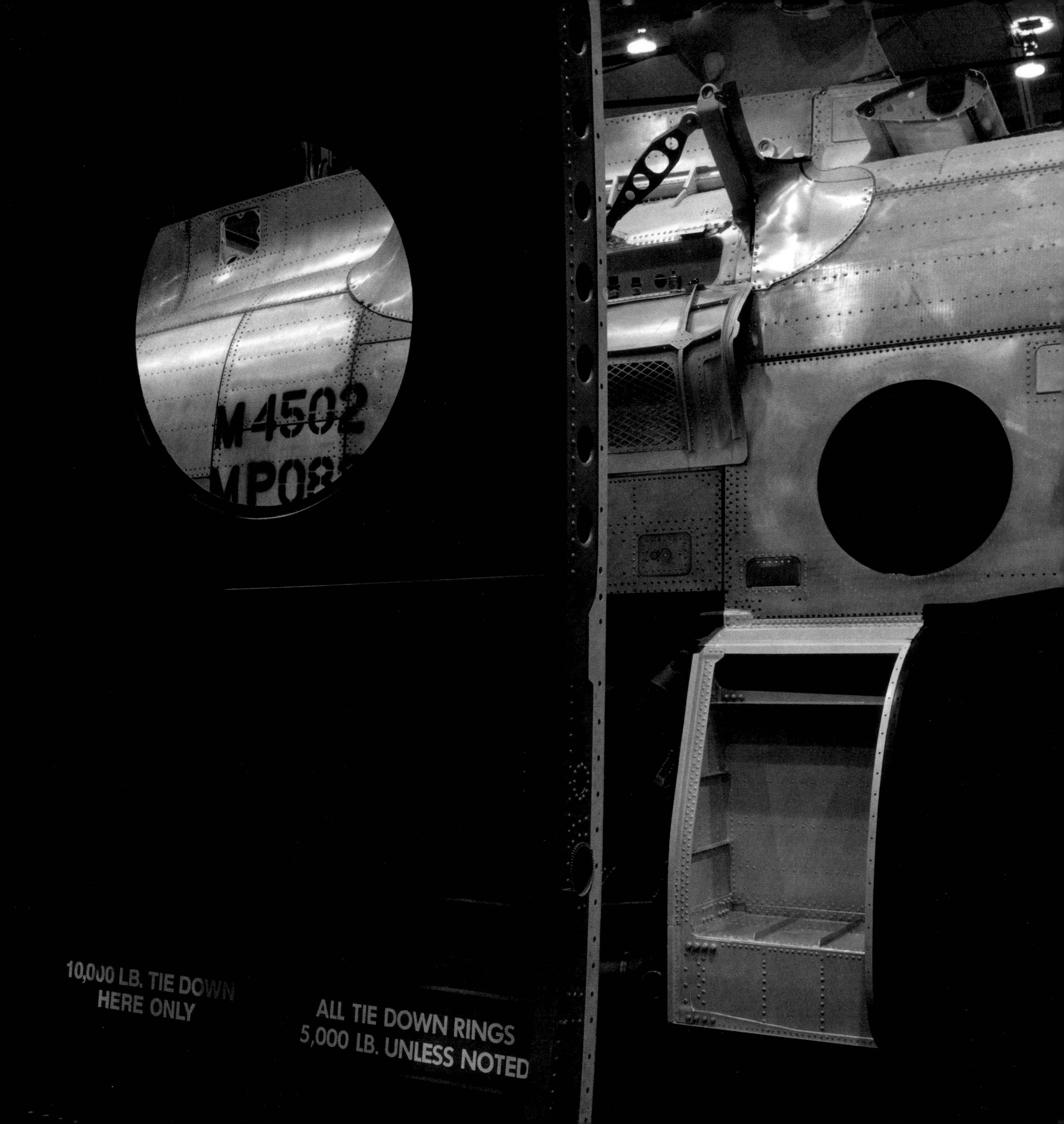

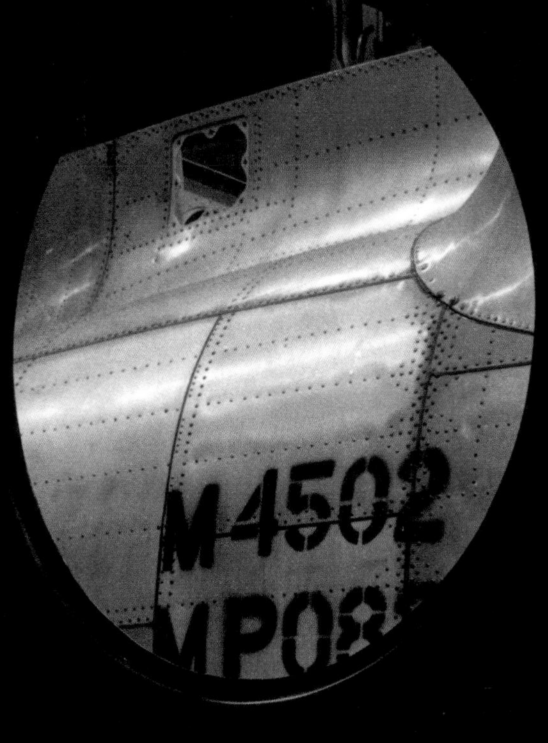
M4502
10,000 LB. TIE DOWN
HERE ONLY
ALL TIE DOWN RINGS
5,000 LB. UNLESS NOTED

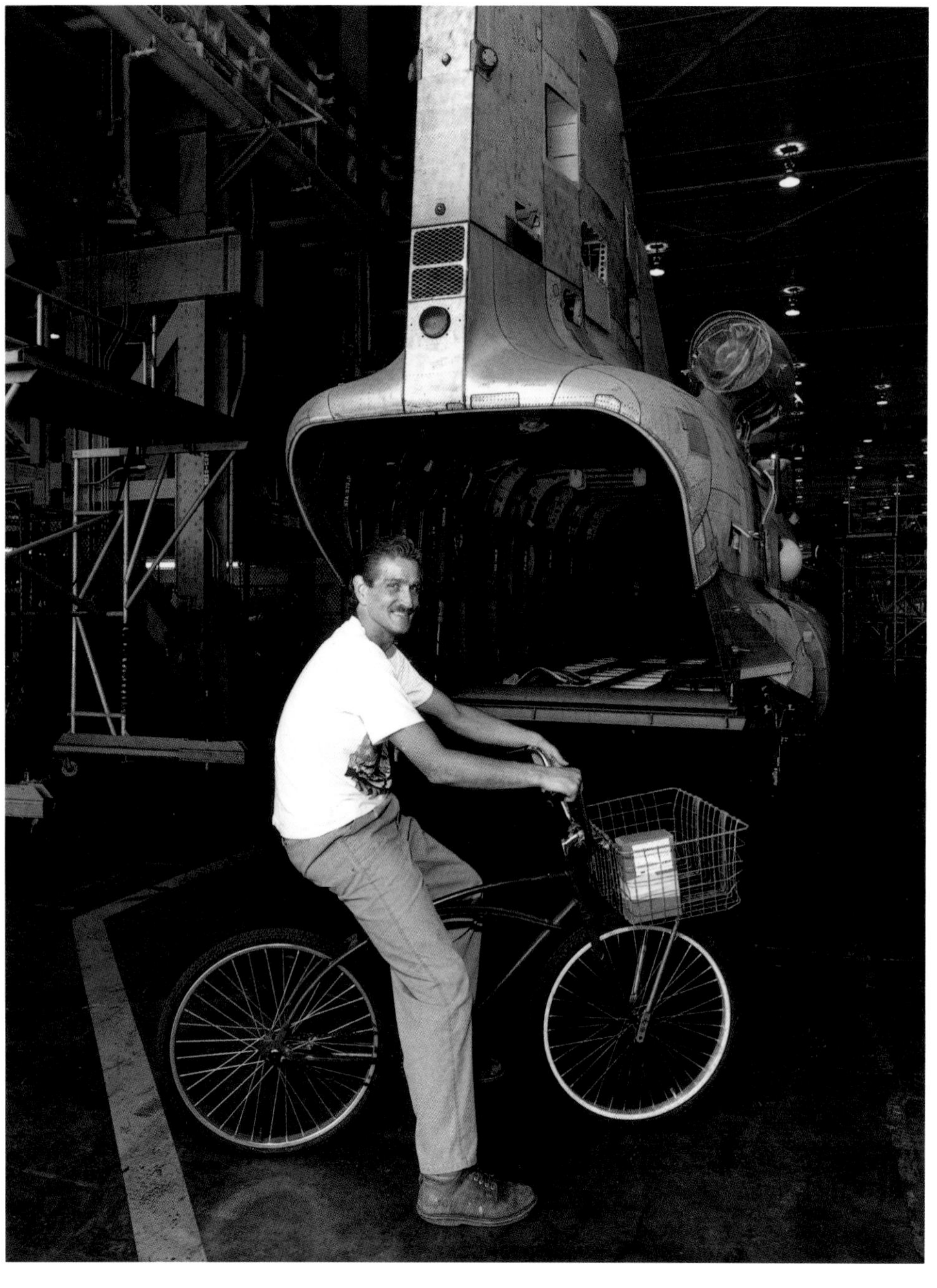

MIKE MAGANNAGO RUNS ERRANDS ON THE SPRAWLING SHOP FLOOR BY BICYCLE.

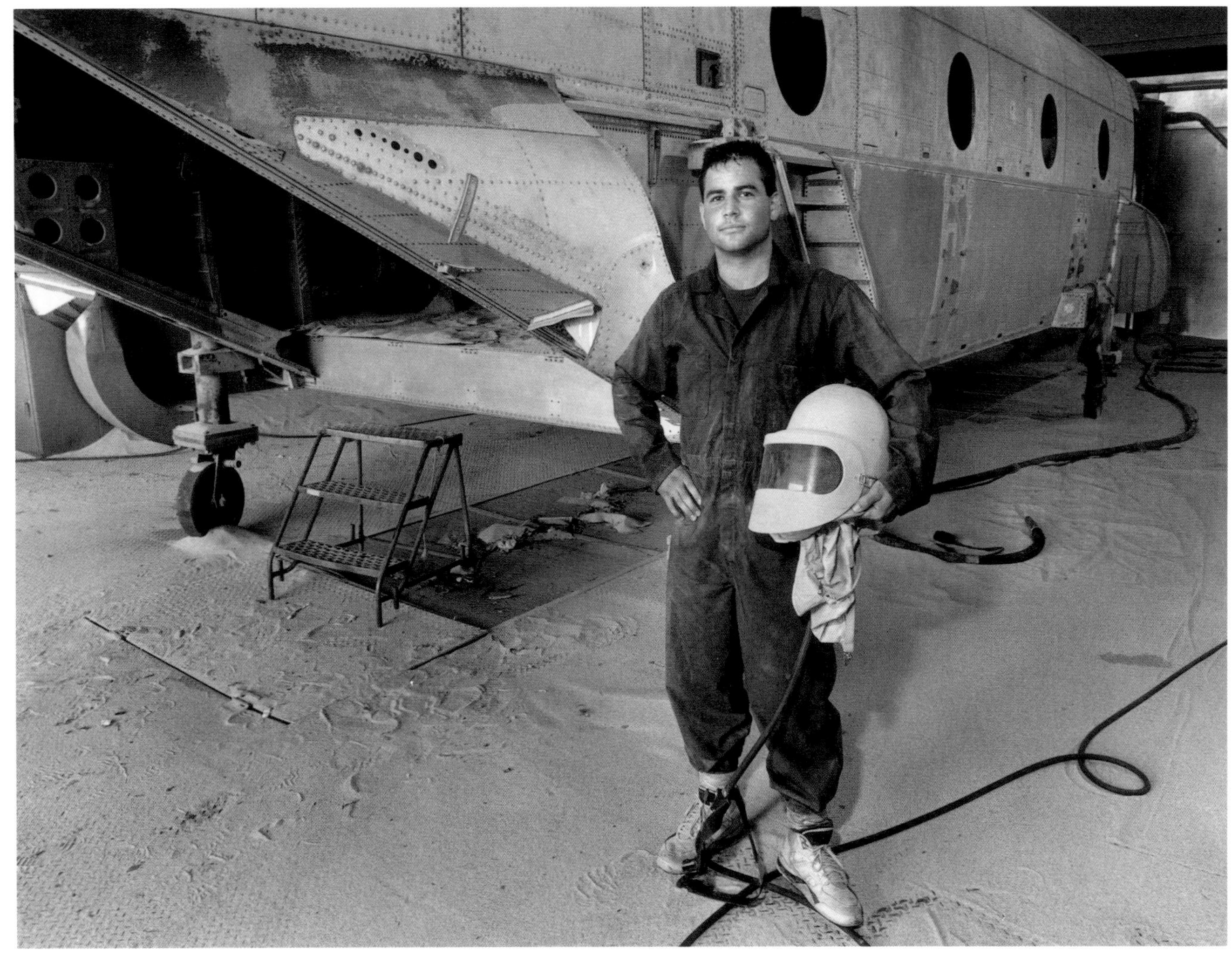

PETE KEENAN, BLASTER, PAUSES FROM REMOVING PAINT AND GREASE FROM CHINOOKS.

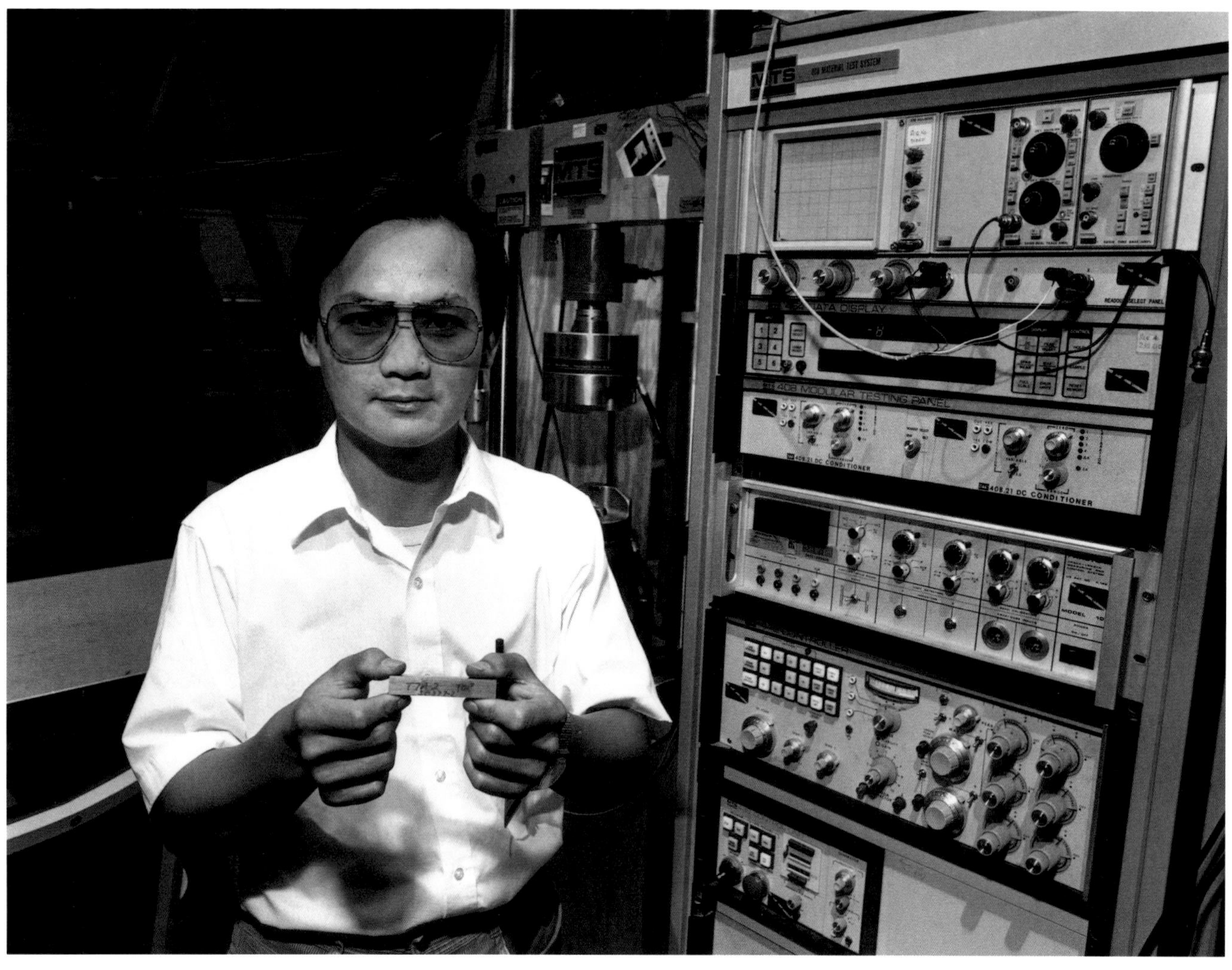

NHIEN NGUYEN TESTS MATERIALS IN THE ENGINEERING TEST LABORATORY.

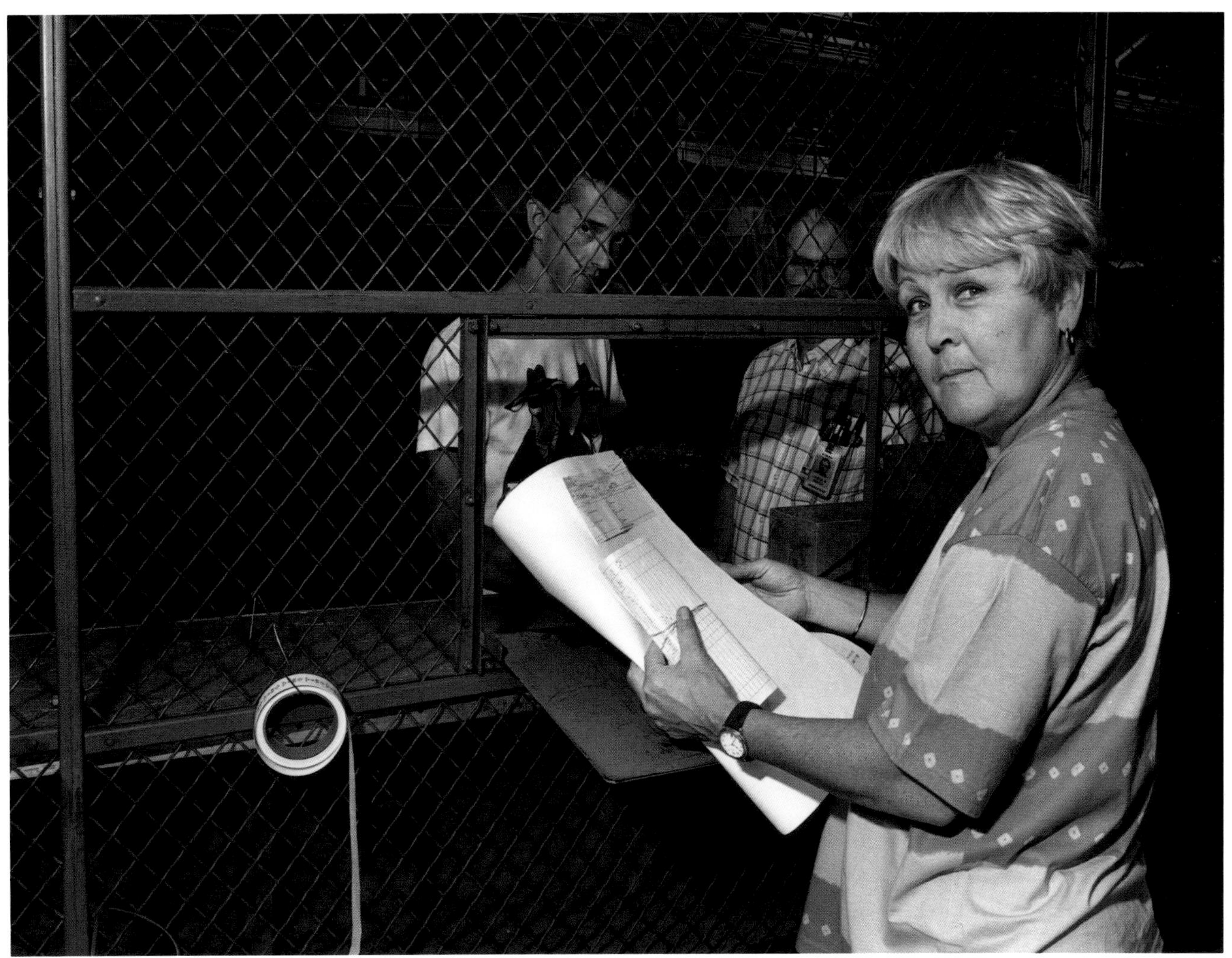

JOAN STARZINSKI
IN BLUEPRINT ROOM OF
THE CHINOOK "D"
MODIFICATION LINE.

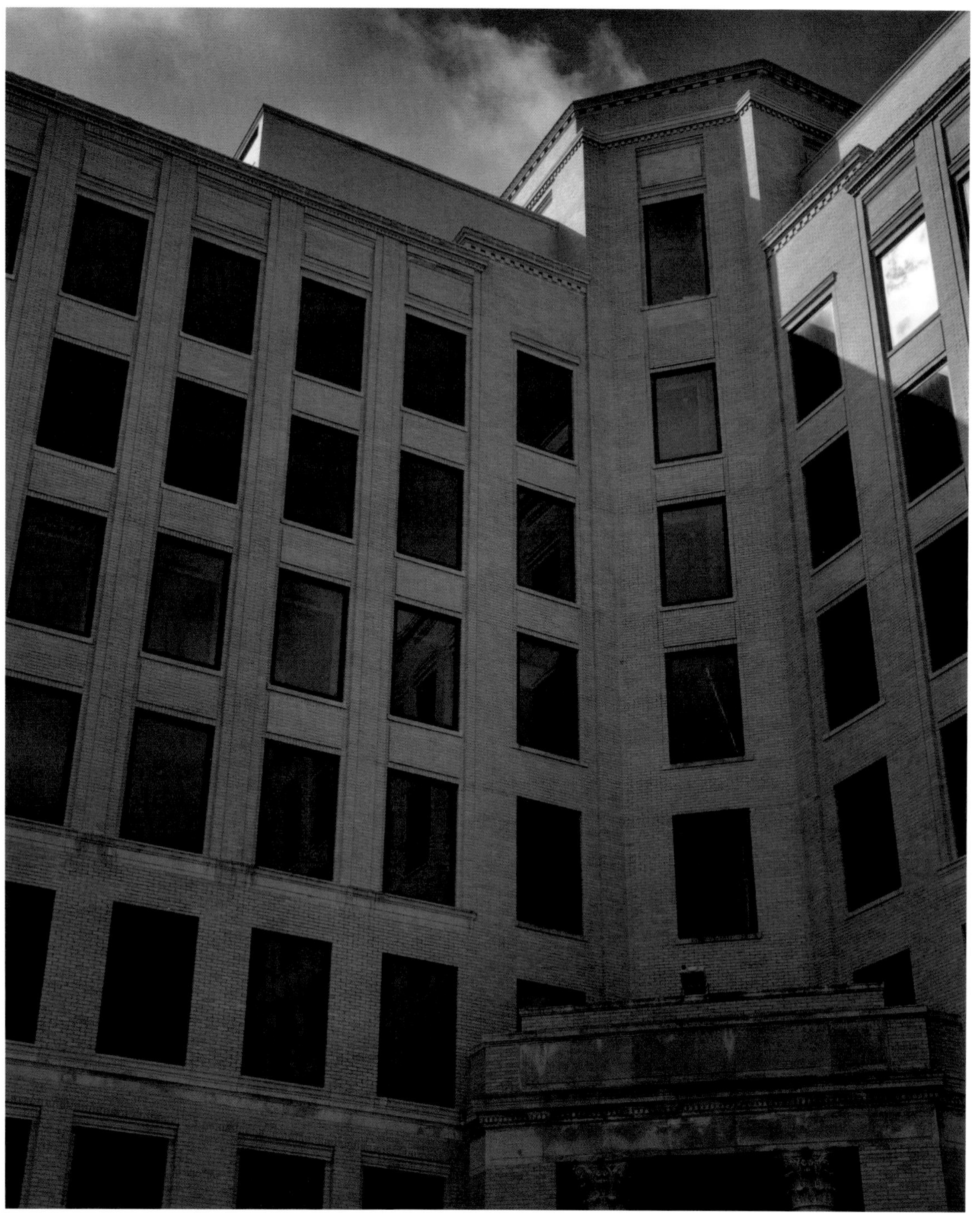

BALDWIN'S EDDYSTONE ADMINISTRATION BUILDING WAS BUILT IN 1928.

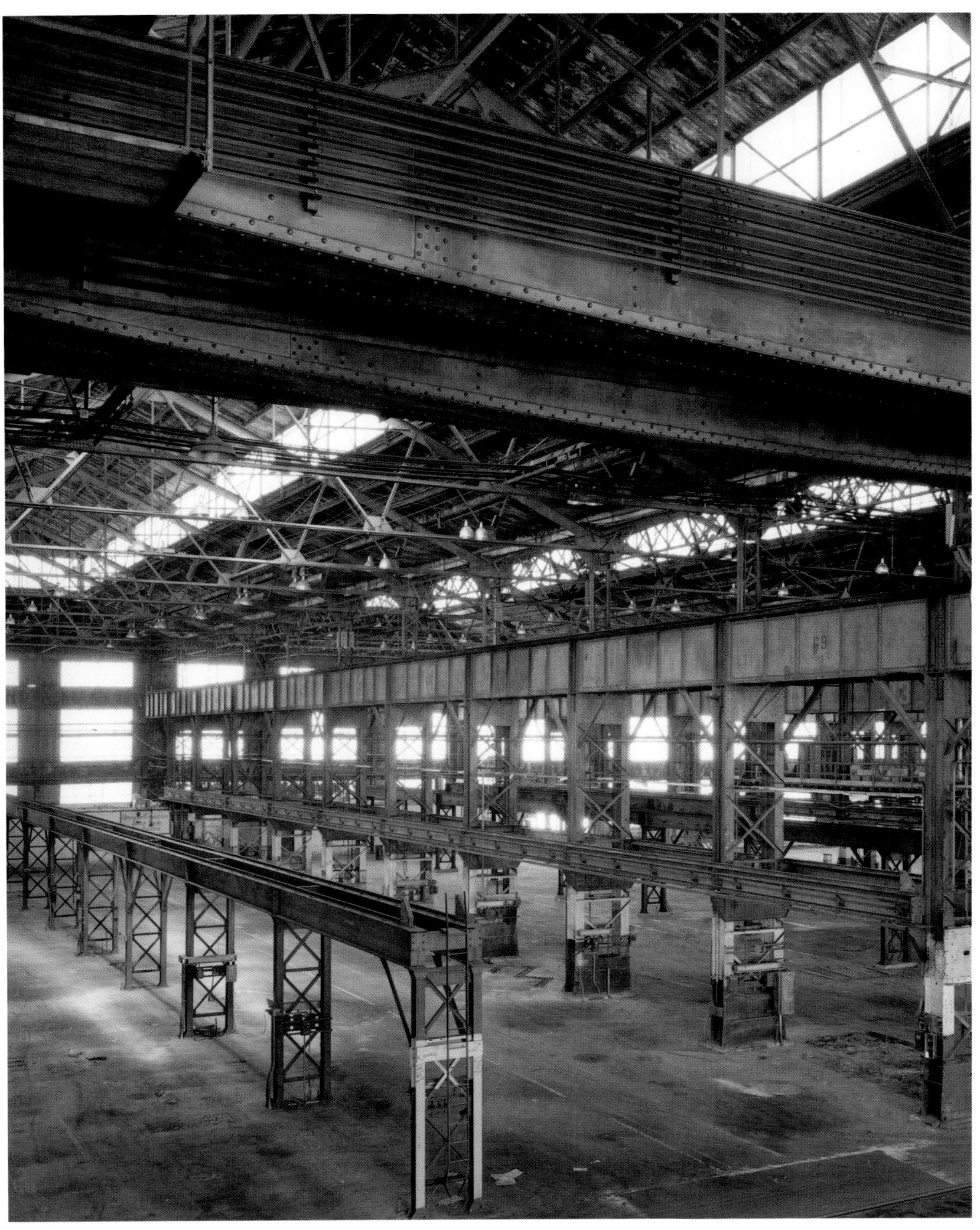

BALDWIN'S SECTION "A" ERECTING SHOP COVERS AN AREA EQUAL TO TEN FOOTBALL FIELDS.

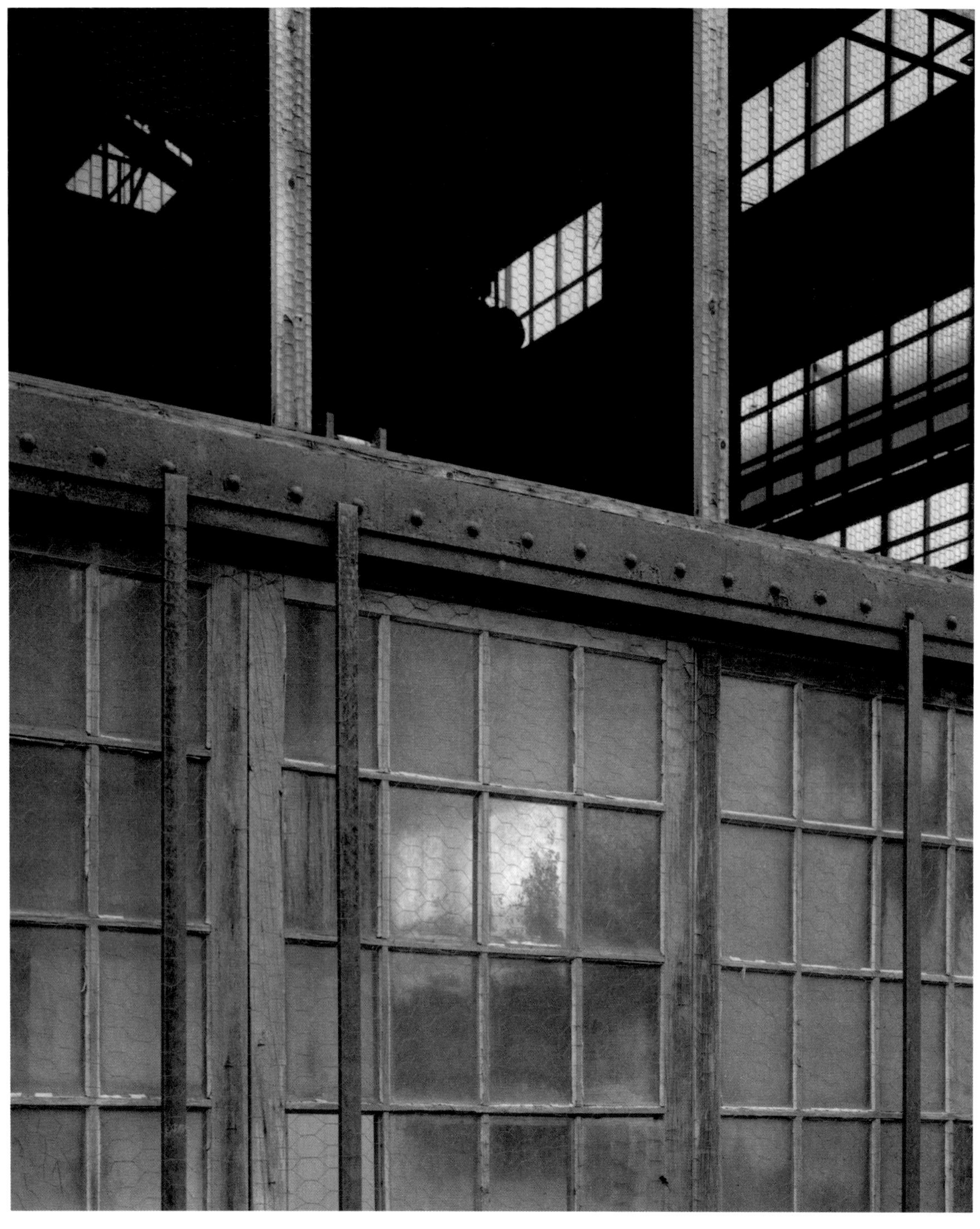

EXTERIOR DETAIL OF THE SECTION "A" ERECTING SHOP AT EDDYSTONE.

RIGHT: SMOKEBOX FRONT OF PENNSYLVANIA RAILROAD FREIGHT LOCOMOTIVE, BUILT BY BALDWIN IN 1916.

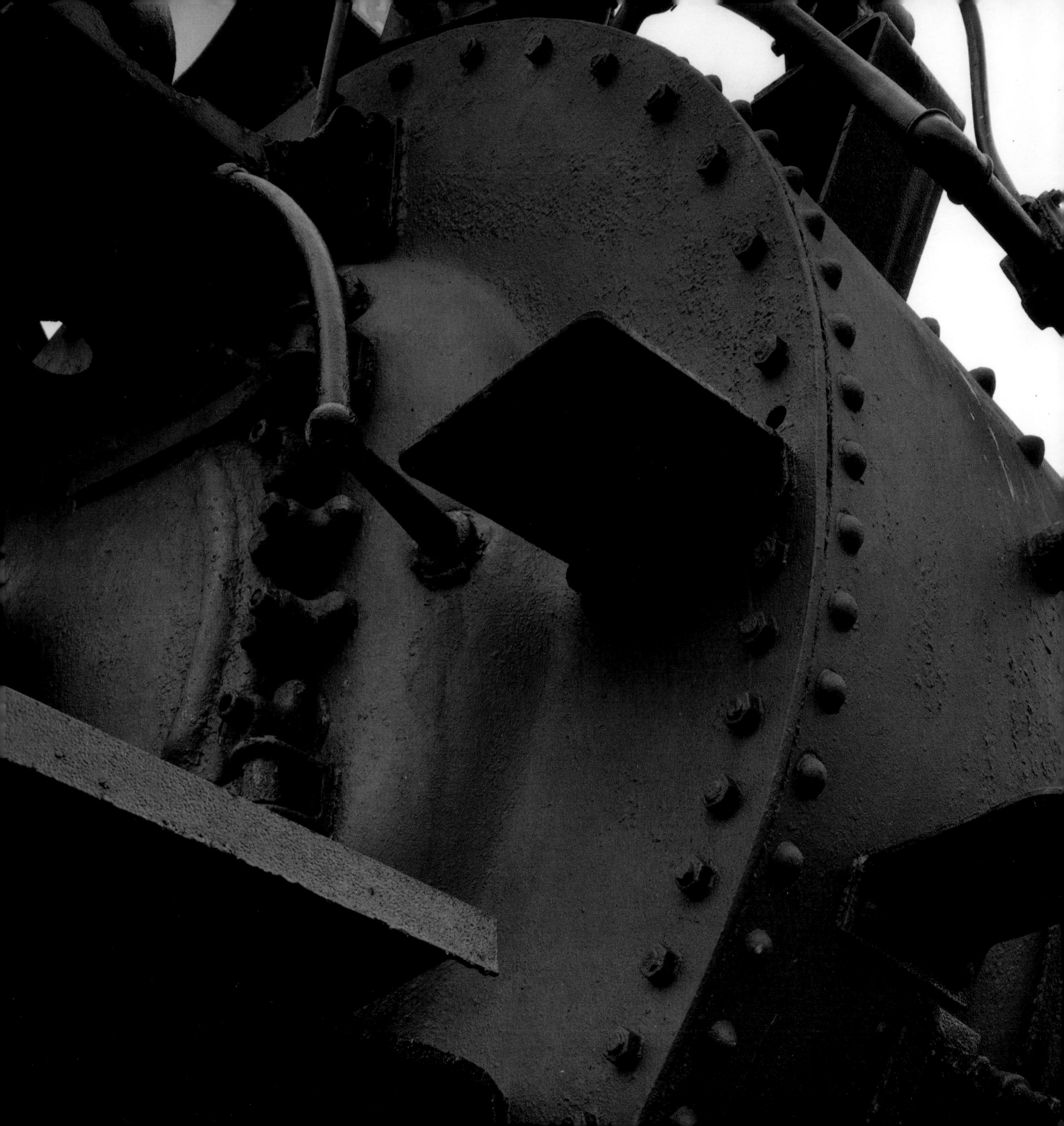

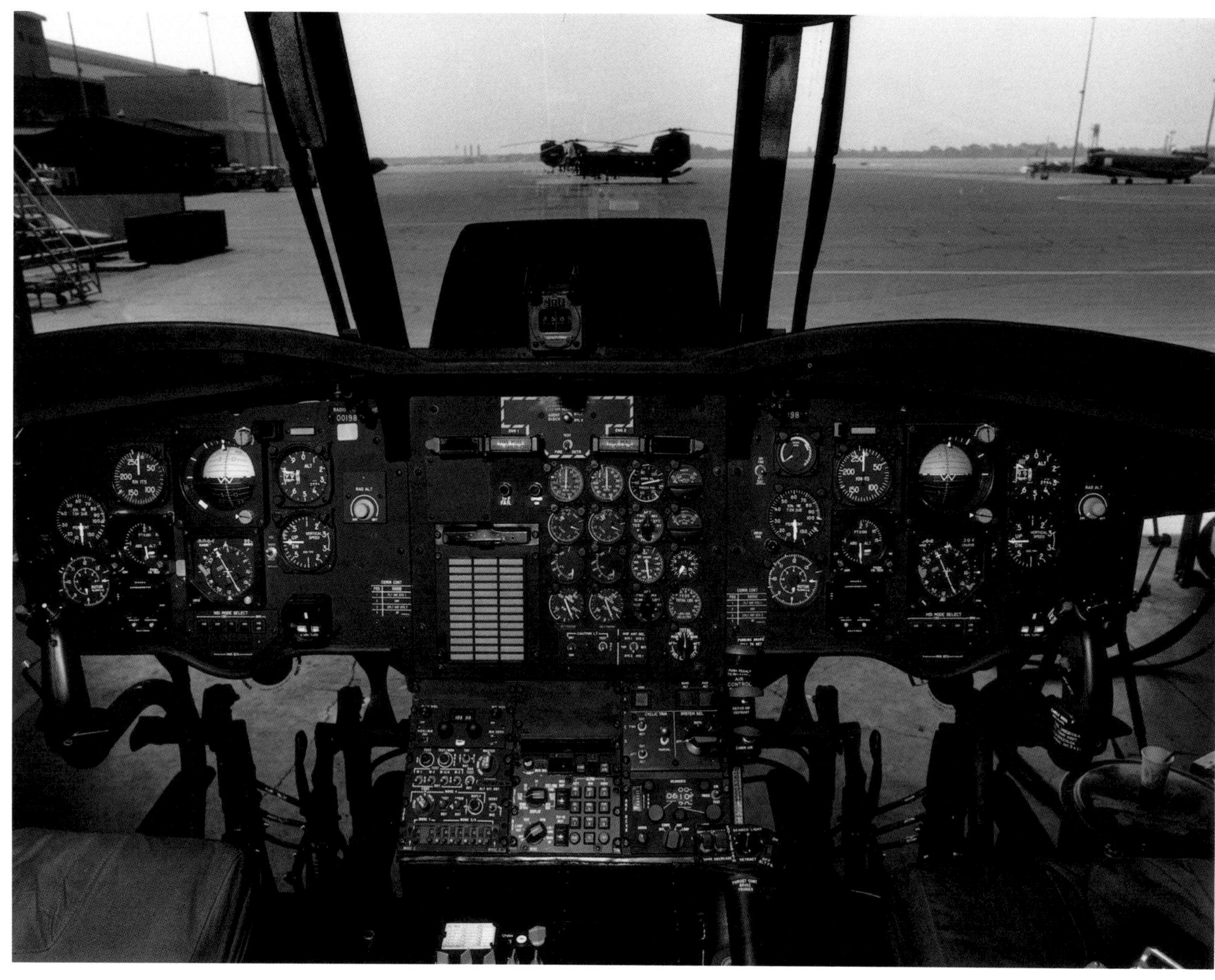

COCKPIT VIEW FROM A COMPLETED CHINOOK LOOKING OUT TOWARD THE FLIGHT RAMP.

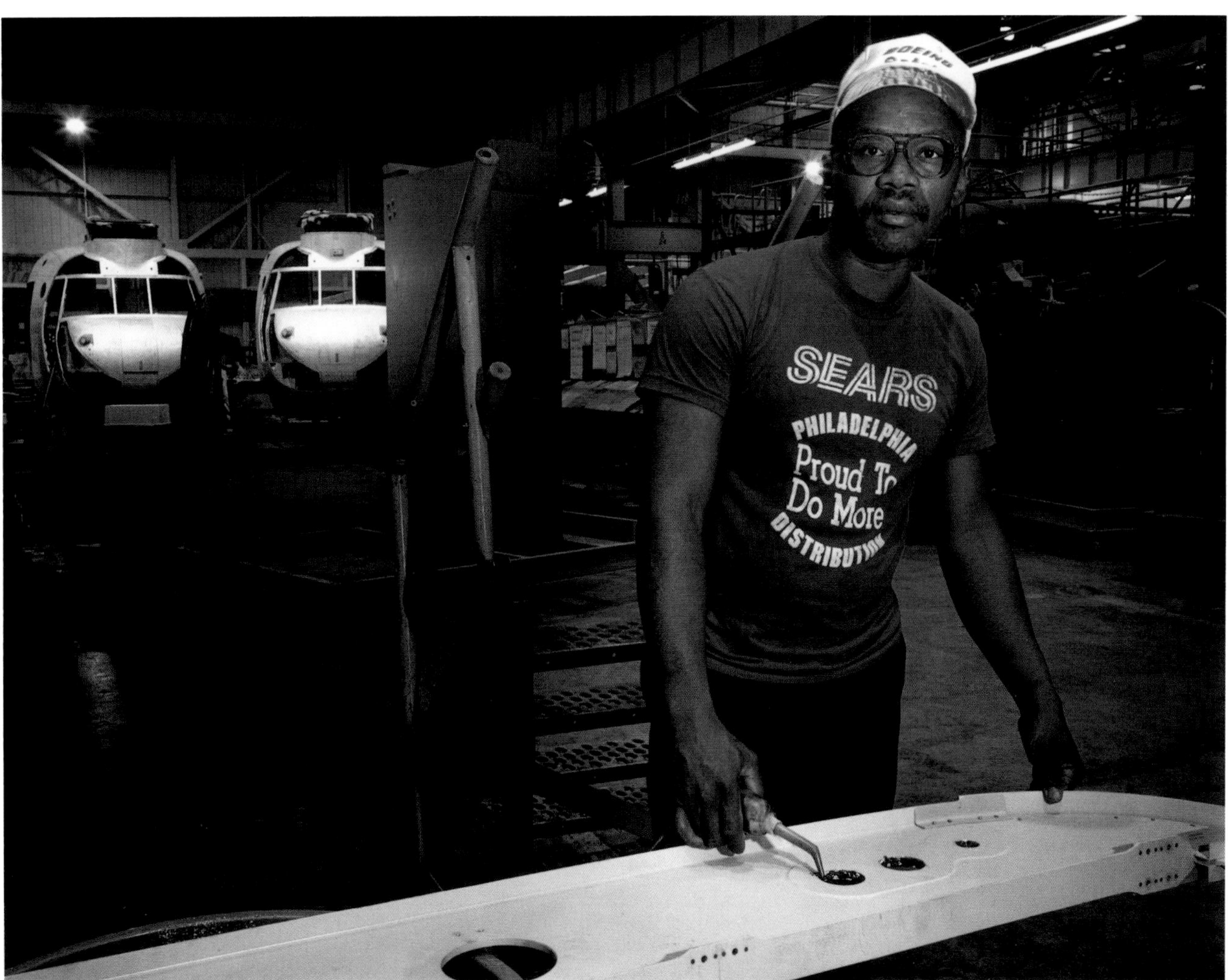

KENNETH SETTLES SEALS A FLOOR BEAM FOR A CHINOOK HELICOPTER.

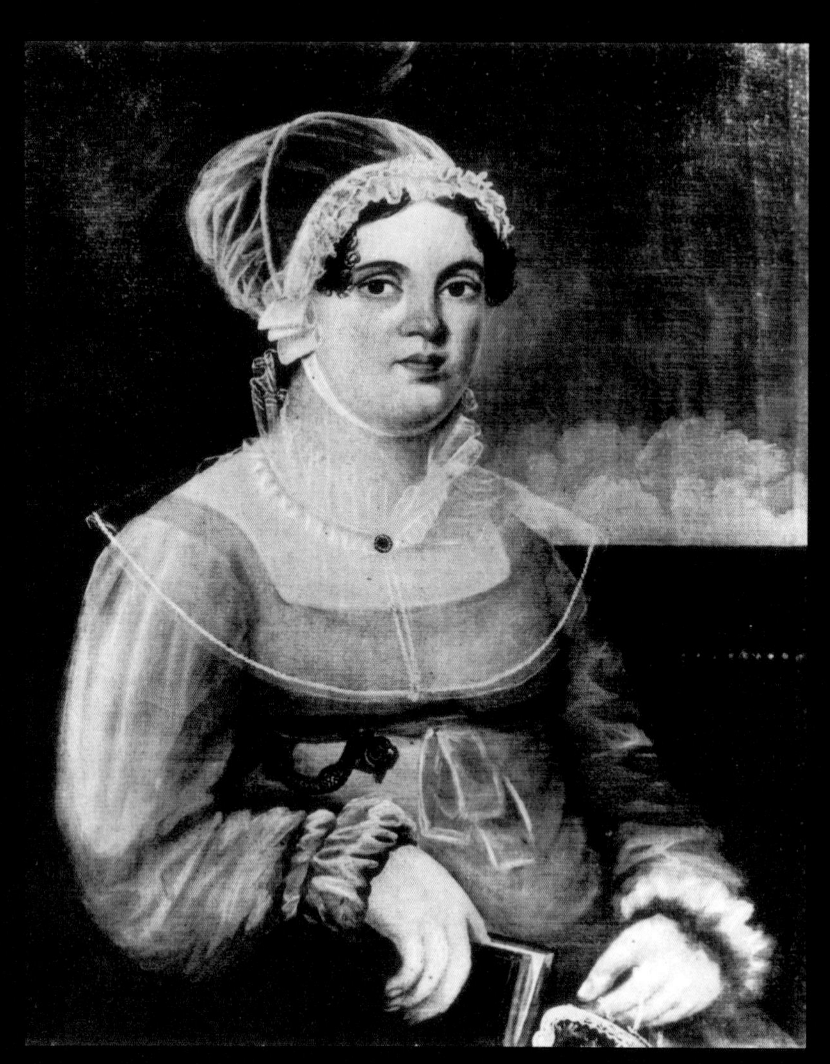

SURVIVAL THROUGH SPECIALIZATION:

THE LUKENS STORY

REBECCA WEBB LUKENS (1794–1854), ONE OF AMERICA'S FIRST BUSINESS WOMEN, SUCCESSFULLY OPERATED HER HUSBAND'S ROLLING MILL FROM HIS PREMATURE DEATH IN 1825, UNTIL 1847.

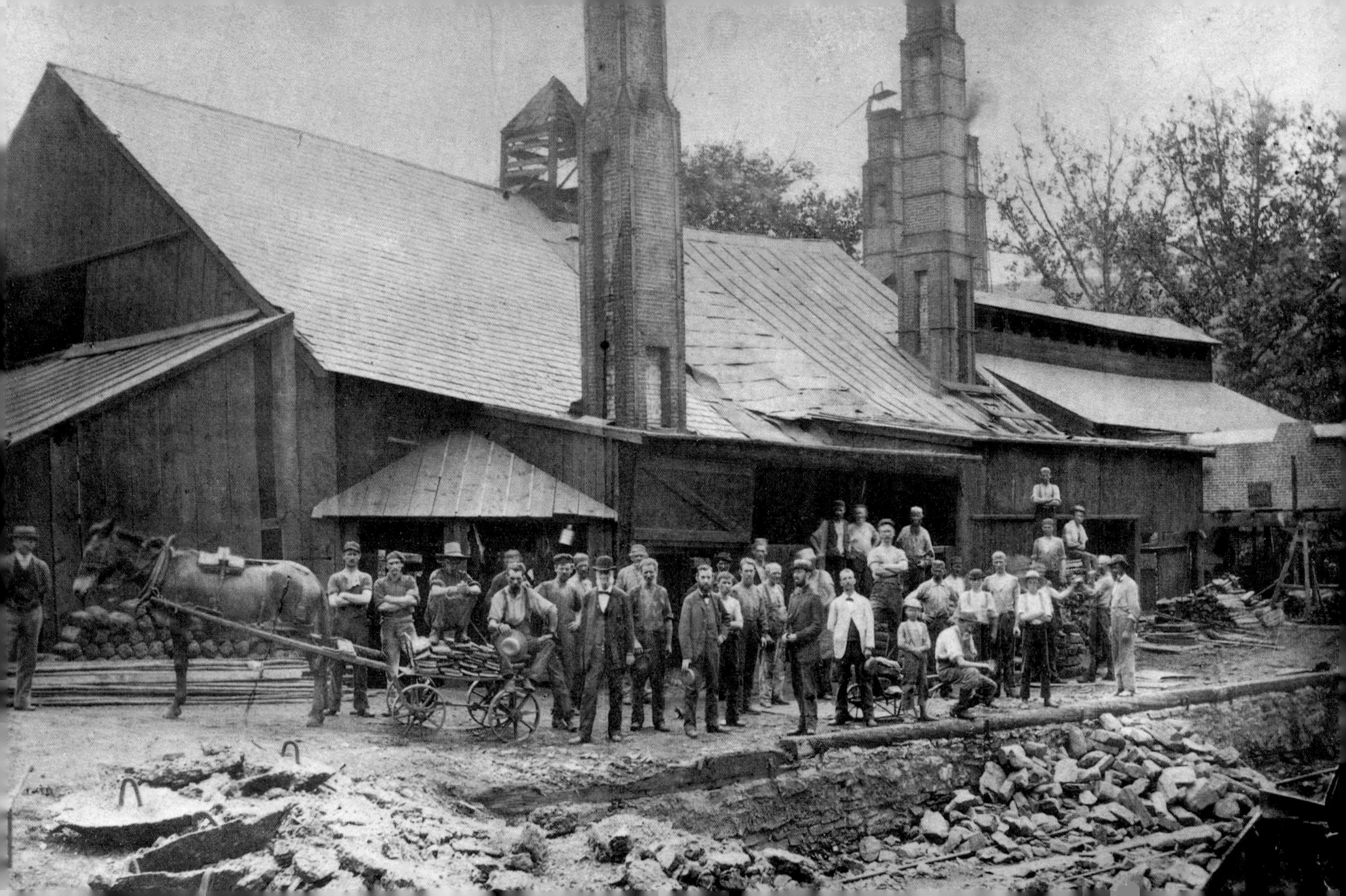

Lukens Steel of Coatesville, Pennsylvania, is virtually the only survivor of the many medium-sized iron and steel works that once dotted the lower Delaware Valley. Occupying the same site for more than 180 years, it has succeeded by developing expertise in a particular product line—steel plates and alloy steels.

Isaac Pennock, a young Quaker entrepreneur who had built the Federal Slitting Mill about four miles south of Coatesville in the 1790s, moved his operation to the site in 1810, naming it the Brandywine Iron Works and Nail Factory. At the works, iron obtained from nearby forges was rolled into sheets and then slit into rods that were sold to blacksmiths or cut into nails. Pennock's son-in-law, Dr. Charles Lukens, entered the business in 1816. The firm rolled the first boiler plate in America in 1818.

After Dr. Lukens' early death in 1825, the operation was directed by his widow, Rebecca Webb (Pennock) Lukens, the first woman in the United States to manage an iron works. She brought the firm through the boom-and-bust years of the 1830s and 1840s and saw the business well established before her death in 1854. In 1850 she remarked that, "There were many causes to make me an object of jealous observers: I had built a very superior mill, though a plain one, and our character for making boiler iron stood first in the market, hence we had as much business as we could do, prices were then good."

Lukens had brought in her sons-in-law, Abraham Gibbons, Jr. and Dr. Charles Huston, as her successors. In 1859 the works were renamed the Lukens Rolling Mill in honor of Dr. and Mrs. Lukens. Control of the business passed to their descendants in the Huston family, first to Dr. Huston and then to his two sons, Abram F. Huston and Charles Lukens Huston. The firm was incorporated as the Lukens Iron and Steel Company in 1890, reorganizing and re-incorporating as the Lukens Steel Company in 1917. The retirement of Charles Lukens Huston, Jr. in 1974 finally ended more than 180 years of direct family management.

Although more than 100 years of technical improvements have radically transformed the scale and productivity of the enterprise, the manufacture of iron or steel plate has remained basically the same over the years. Hot metal slabs are passed and repassed through a series of rollers until they are flattened into a plate of the desired width and thickness. The extremes of temperature and the fluctuating din of the plates rattling over the rollers have remained a constant fact of life in a rolling mill. The work traditionally has required a combination of physical strength and the ability to gauge the quality of metal by its color and "feel." The less skilled jobs involved handling the heavy raw materials, stoking furnaces, and manipulating the plates at the end of the rolling process. As a result, this was unashamedly "man's work" until relatively recently as chemical and metallurgical analysis have replaced the ironmaster's intuition, and electrification and automation have reduced the need for raw muscle power on the mill floor. Women first entered the mills as a temporary measure during World War II, but have been employed regularly since the 1970s.

Under Rebecca Lukens, the mill was a small enterprise that struggled to turn out 500 tons a year. Dr. Huston and his sons transformed it into a nationally-known specialty manufacturer. In 1870 Huston constructed a new 84-inch mill powered by steam, and

THE ORIGINAL ROLLING MILL, SHOWN HERE AROUND 1887, AFTER IT HAD BEEN CONVERTED TO A PUDDLE MILL. IT OPERATED UNTIL 1906 AND WAS LEFT STANDING UNTIL THE LATE 1920S.

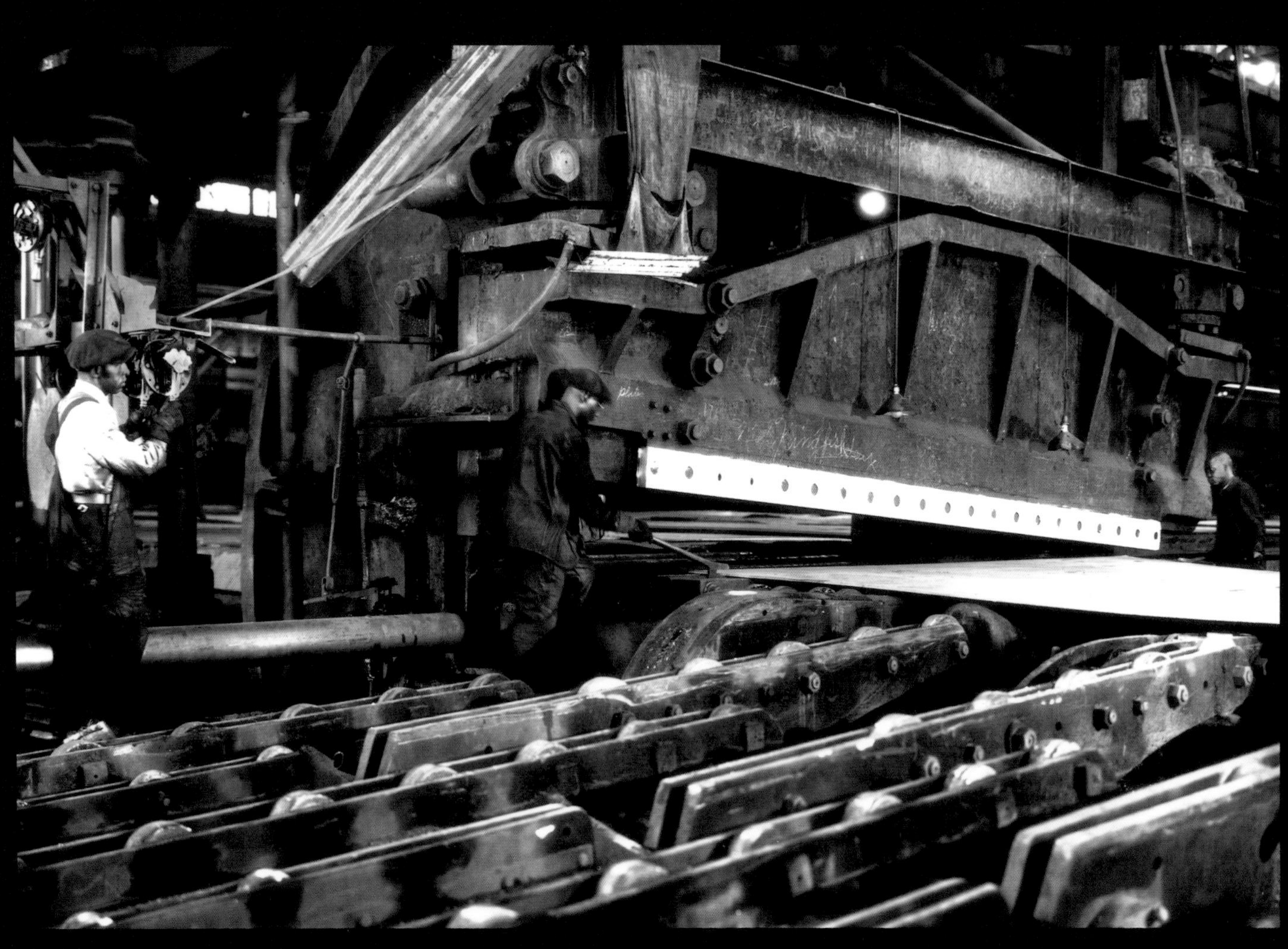

the old mill was converted to puddle rolls to prepare the stock for final rolling. The new mill produced wide plates for the iron shipbuilders of Wilmington. The first steel was rolled in 1880. Charles L. Huston designed and installed a 120-inch universal plate mill for the purpose of rolling mild steel. Open-hearth furnaces, allowing the company to make its own steel, went into production in 1892, and a 140-inch mill was added in 1902. Huston also designed the 206-inch mill that was installed in 1918. This was the largest plate mill in the world for many years and was capable of rolling plates up to twenty-five inches thick and more than sixteen feet wide.

Lukens first built its reputation by manufacturing boiler iron since the industrializing of steam-powered America required increasing numbers of ever-stronger boilers and fireboxes. In 1885 the firm installed its first head-spinning machine which permitted the soft-forming of dished or hemispherical heads for boilers and pressure vessels.

Although Lukens remained a relatively small company and never attempted to become a fully-integrated steel company, it did take some steps in that direction. In 1907 it purchased a controlling interest in the Alleghany Ore & Iron Company, operating three iron furnaces at Iron Gate, Buena Vista, and Shenandoah, Virginia, and iron ore mines at Oriskany, Virginia. In the twentieth century, Lukens integrated forward to include the preliminary shaping and finishing of plates.

Lukens expanded its product line in 1927 by forming a subsidiary, the By-Products Steel Corporation, to manufacture a wide range of sheared, blanked, and pressed shapes from steel plate. A second subsidiary, Lukenweld, Inc., was formed in 1930 to cut and fabricate shapes from steel plate by arc welding. In the same year, Lukens joined with International Nickel to develop "clad steels," a sandwich of steel plate, heat-and-pressure-coated with corrosion-resistant finishes. These new facilities enabled Lukens to switch from steam boilers to supplying newer industries, turning out underframes and crankcases for diesel engines and automotive parts. Clad steel found ready markets in the chemical and petroleum industries, and later in the nuclear industry from the Manhattan Project onward. Lukens' specialty, steel plate, was basic enough to enable the company to prosper, even as its customer industries rose and fell.

Under the first generations of Quaker owners, Lukens had refused to make any products for military use. Temporarily reversed by an outpouring of Union fervor in 1862, this policy was not permanently altered until America entered World War I. During World War II the military became a prime customer and remained so through the 1980s. Lukens steel has been used by the manufacturers of ships, submarines, tanks, and the atomic energy program, including the Abrams Tank, the Bradley Fighting Vehicle, and the Patriot anti-missile missile used in Operation Desert Storm.

In 1944, the peak year of war production, Lukens produced 577,323 tons of steel with a work force numbering 6,315. By then older mills had been scrapped, and natural gas had already replaced coal for fuel. The 206-inch mill was converted from steam to electric drive in 1950. Beginning with the Korean War, production consistently exceeded World War II levels, finally peaking at nearly 958,000 tons in 1974. During this time Lukens modernized its plant, enabling it to

SINCE THE LATE NINETEENTH CENTURY A SUBSTANTIAL PORTION OF THE LUKENS STEEL COMPANY WORK FORCE HAS BEEN AFRICAN AMERICAN. THE "TRIMMER GANG" IS SHOWN CUTTING STEEL PLATE IN THE EARLY 1930S.

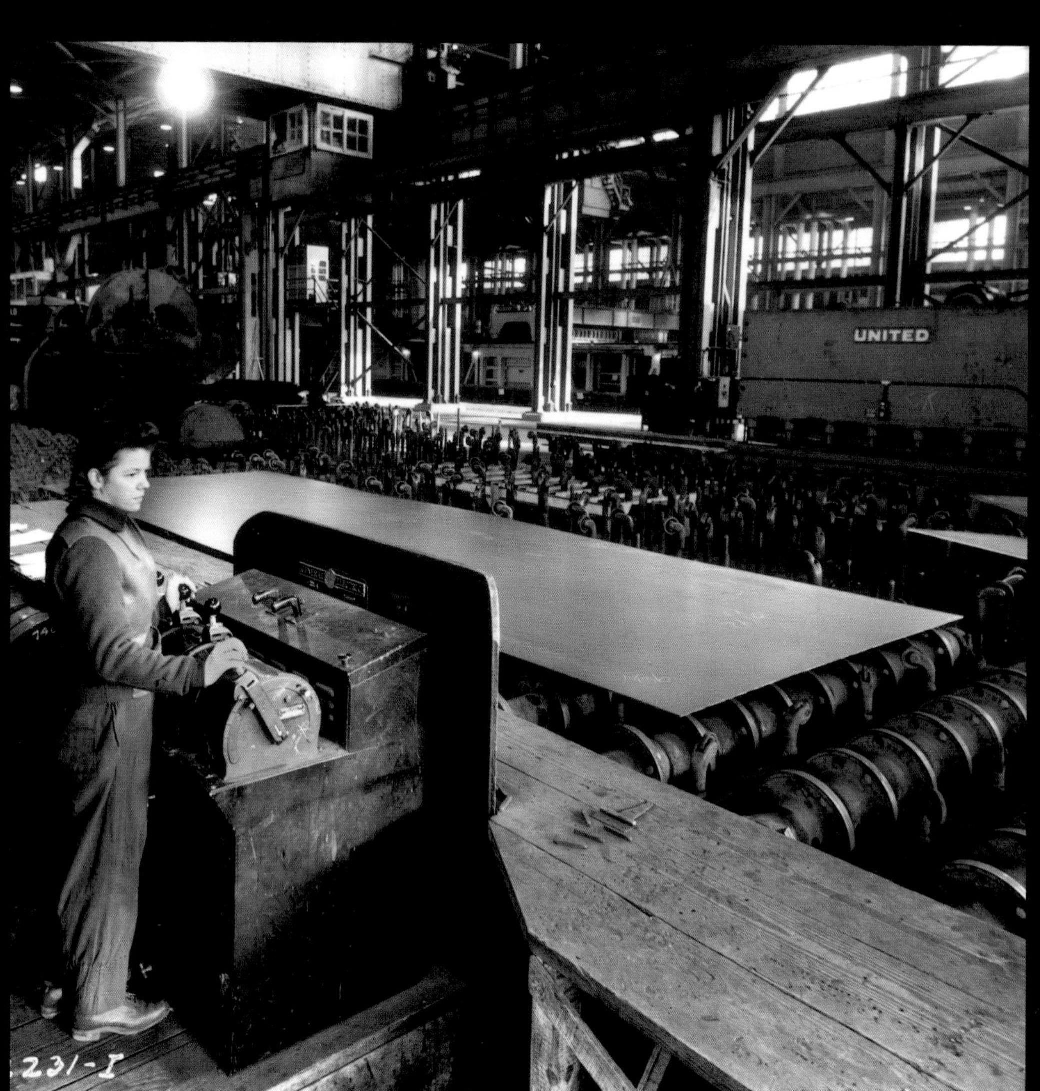
UNITED
231-I

produce nearly 50 percent more steel with almost 20 percent fewer workers. Electric arc furnaces were built in 1958, 1962, 1965, and 1974, and old open hearths were closed in 1975. Lukens installed single-strand slab casting in 1971, permitting direct cast from molten steel, bypassing the ingot stage.

Despite the much-discussed decline of the American steel industry that began in the early 1970s, Lukens has continued to hold its own by investing in new technologies and facilities and in increasing productivity, while most other area steelworks disappeared entirely. Lukens purchased the 110-inch Conshohocken mill of the defunct Alan Wood Steel Company in 1978.

Lukens Steel did not escape the severe industry downturn in the early 1980s, but it fared better than its competitors. Although financial losses occurred and the work force was drastically trimmed in both salaried and hourly ranks, the steelmaker was not burdened with replacing or closing aging and inefficient operations. Earlier investment in modern steelmaking facilities enabled the company to recover faster and take advantage of market opportunities as they arose. The rebuilding of its fourth electric furnace in 1985 with advanced melting technologies and increased power, allowed the company to produce all of its steel needs with one furnace, rather than four. Productivity, measured in tons-per-hour (TPH), was increased from thirty-five TPH to more than 110 TPH. Other steelmaking improvements like ladle refining and increased strand caster speed, further increased productivity while reducing manufacturing costs. These advancements, together with the computerization of its 110-inch and 140-inch rolling mills, made Lukens Steel the low-cost domestic plate steel producer.

IN 1942 WOMEN BEGAN WORKING IN THE STEEL MILLS FOR THE FIRST TIME AS A WAR MEASURE. HERE, A WOMAN STEEL WORKER IS AT THE CONTROLS OF THE 120-INCH MILL.

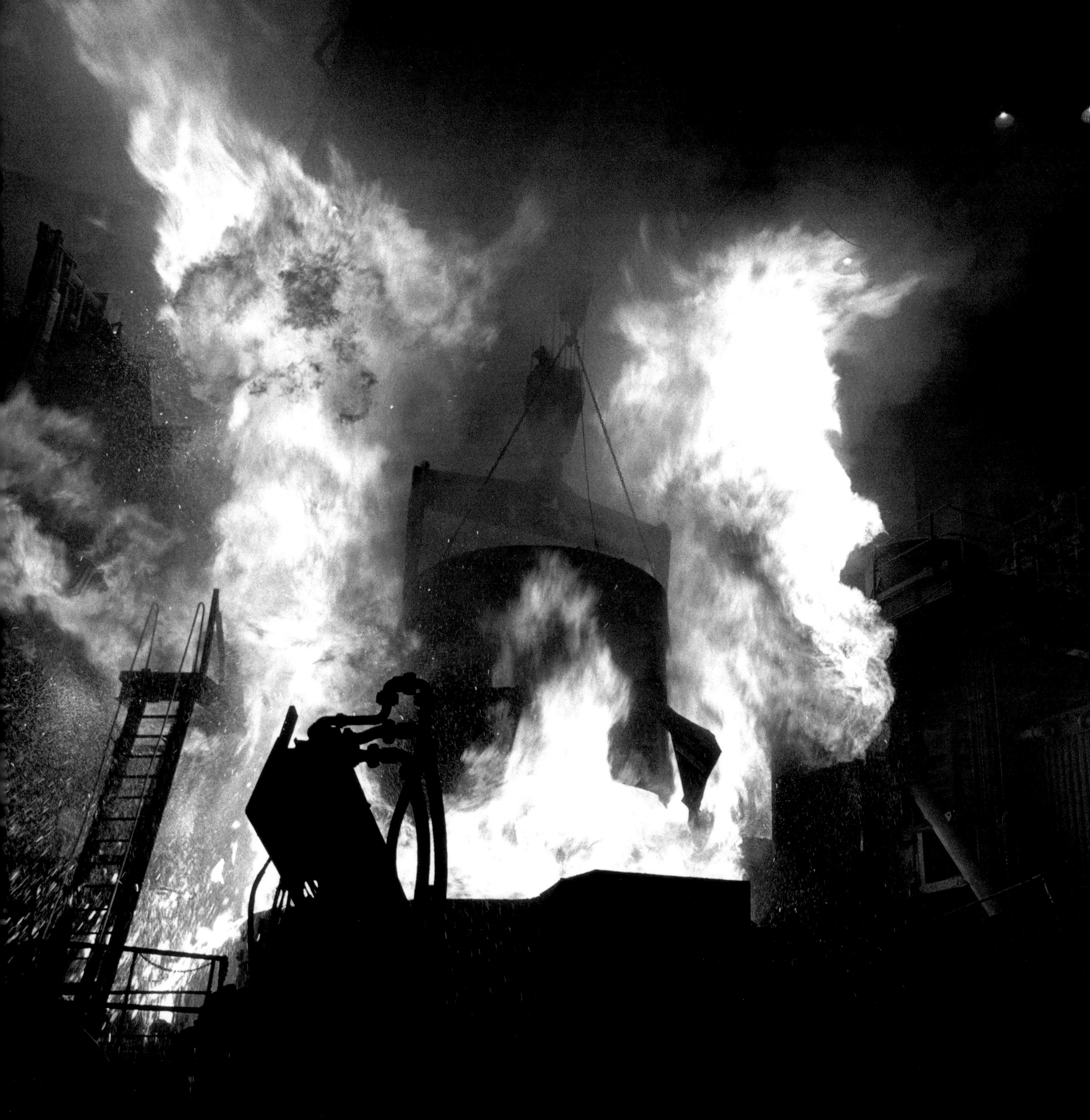

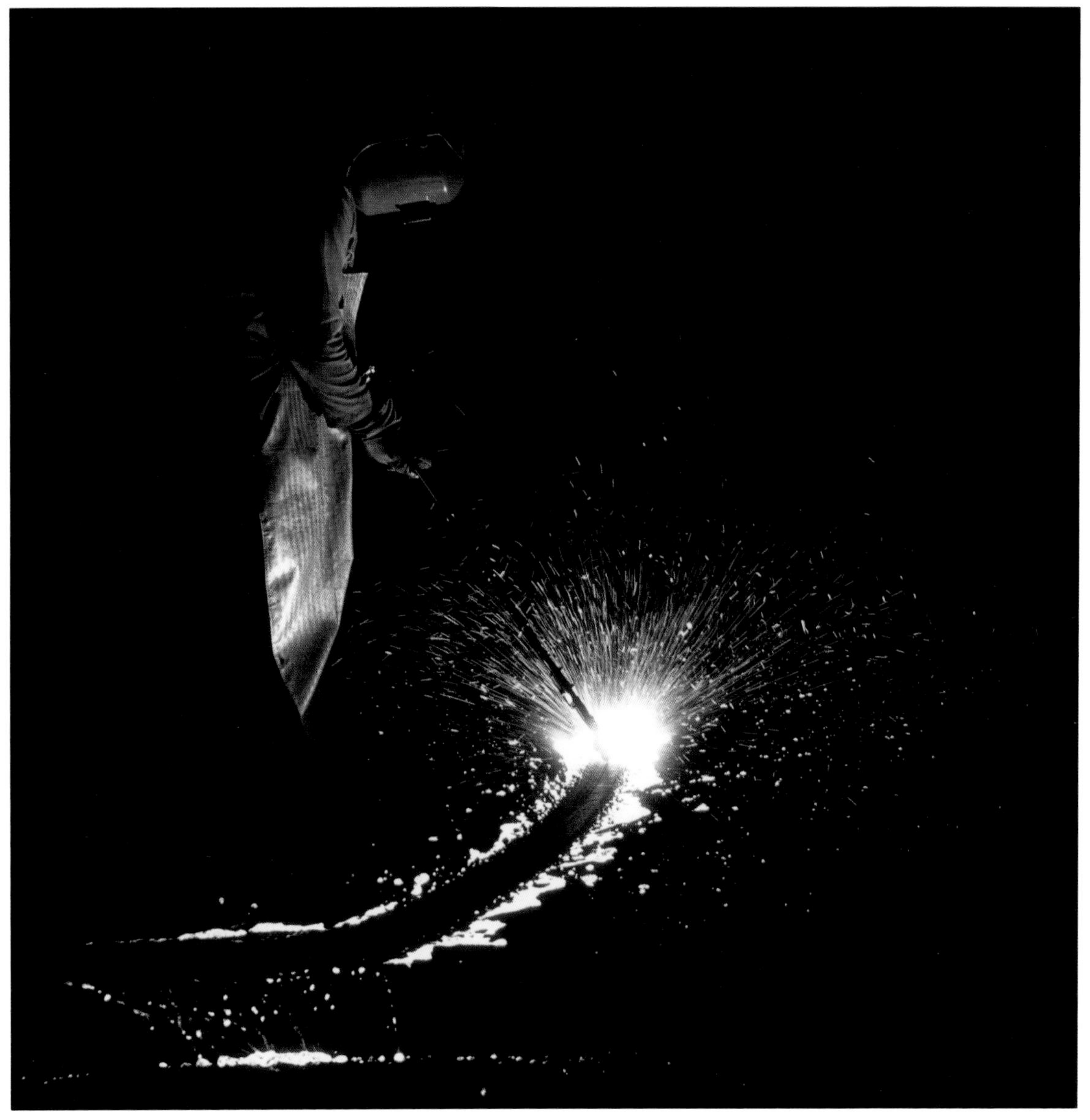

CHARGING AN ELECTRIC ARC FURNACE IN THE ELECTRIC MELT SHOP.

ABOVE: JOHN RAPPOLD DE-SEAMING A SLAB IN THE ALLOY CONDITIONING AREA.

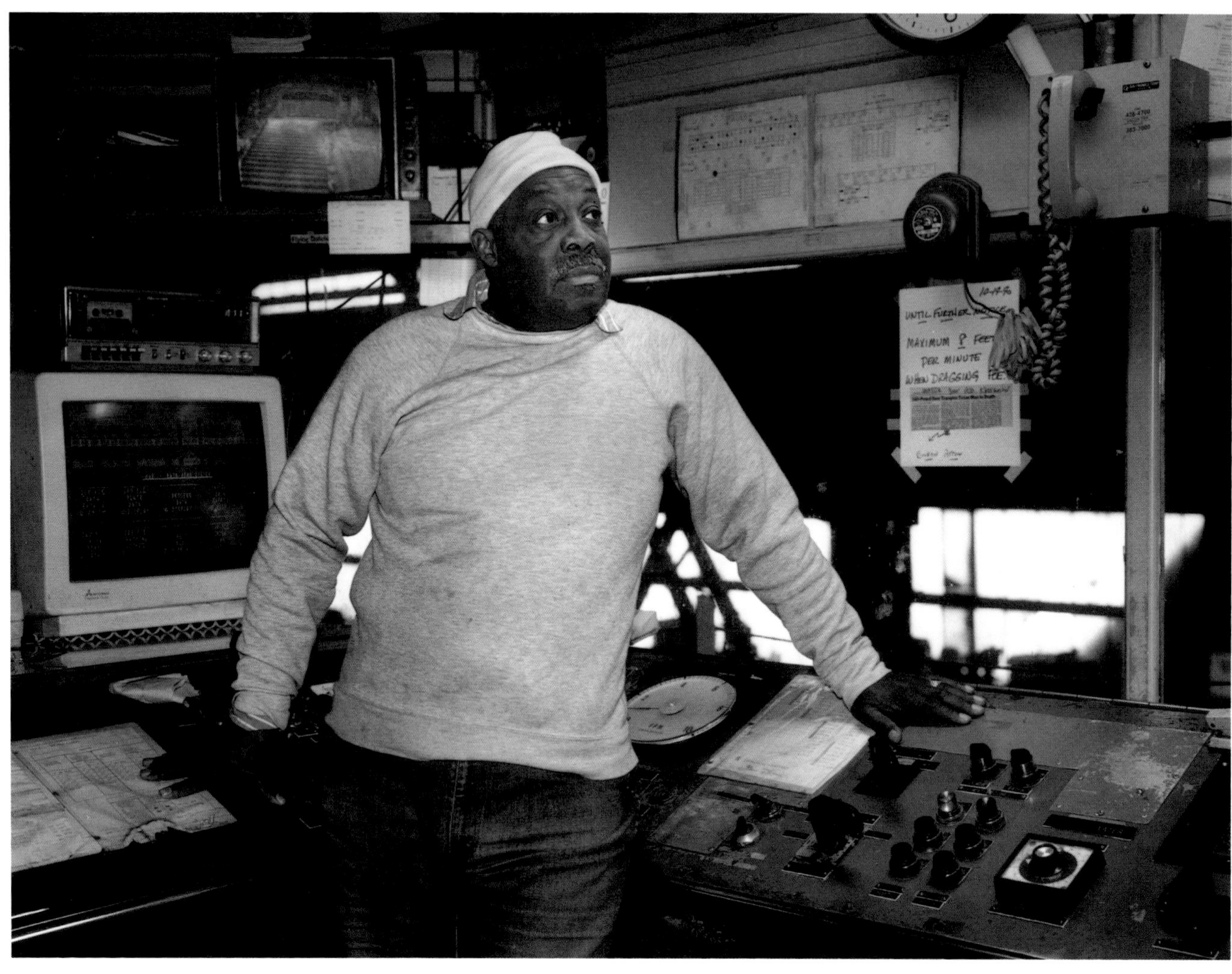

LEON ROLLINS AT THE CONTROL PULPIT FOR THE DREVER FURNACE.

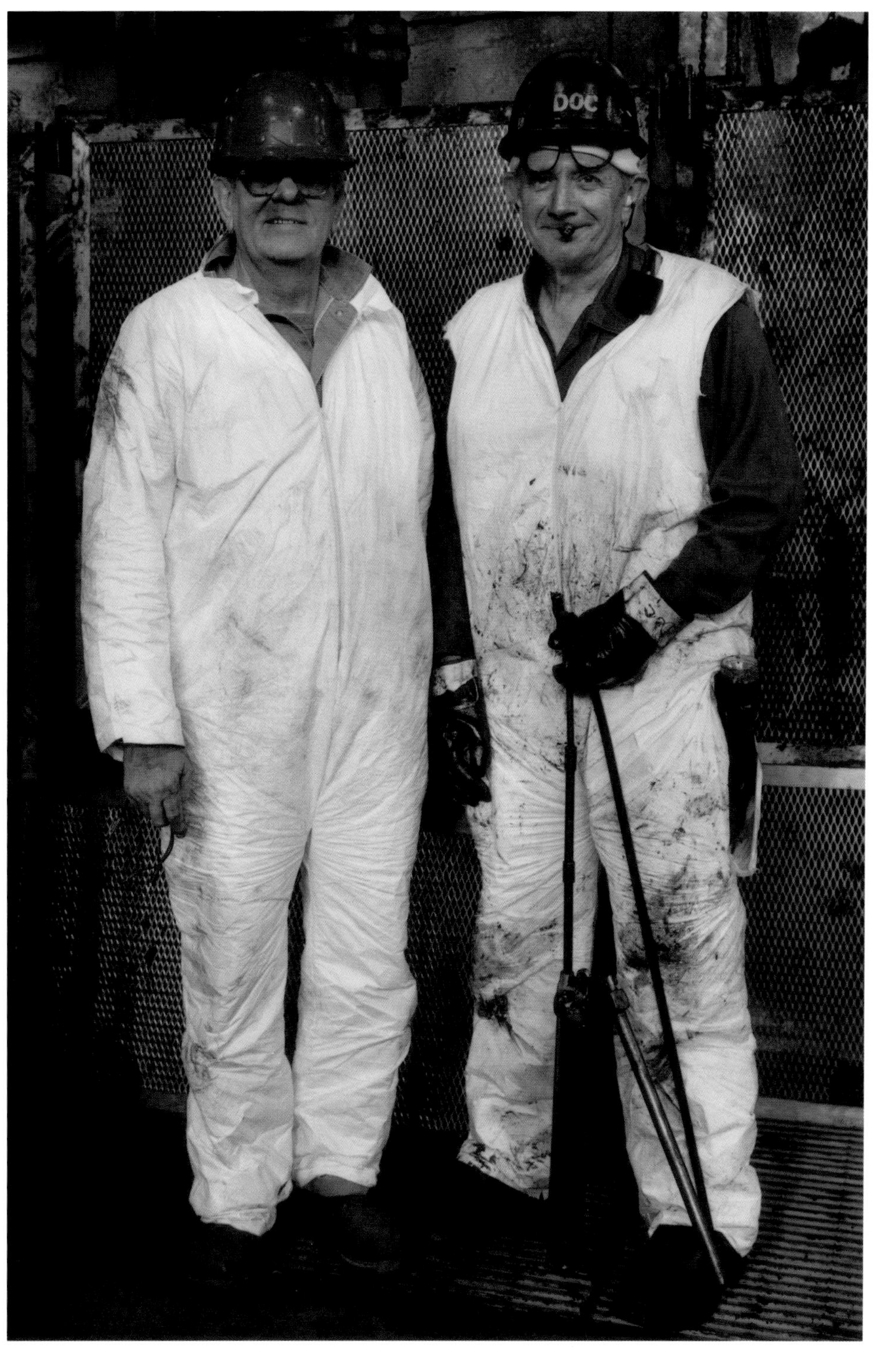

IRVING DE HAVEN AND MICHAEL ZEVTCHIN, MAINTENANCE WORKERS, AT THE DREVER FURNACE.

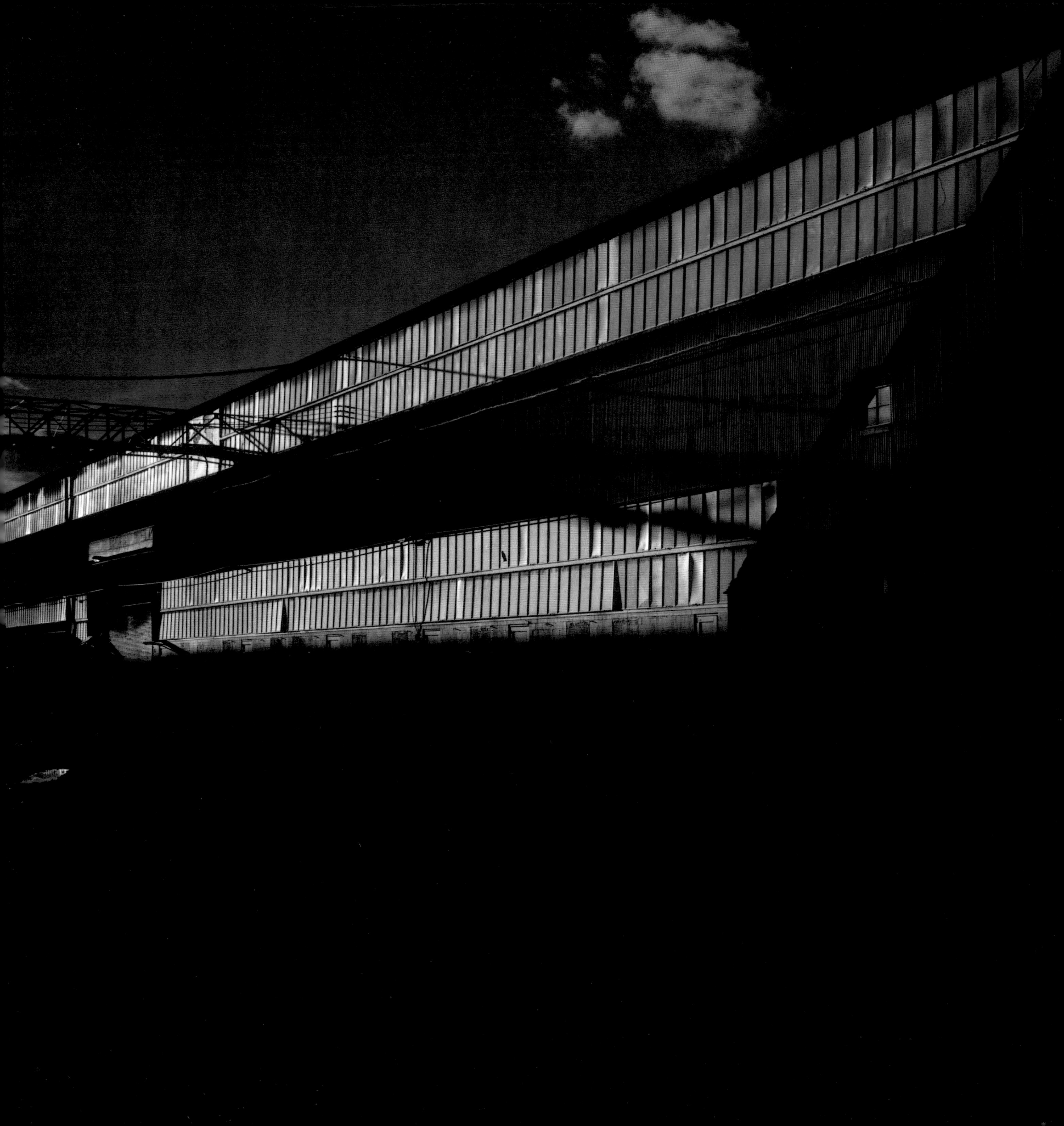

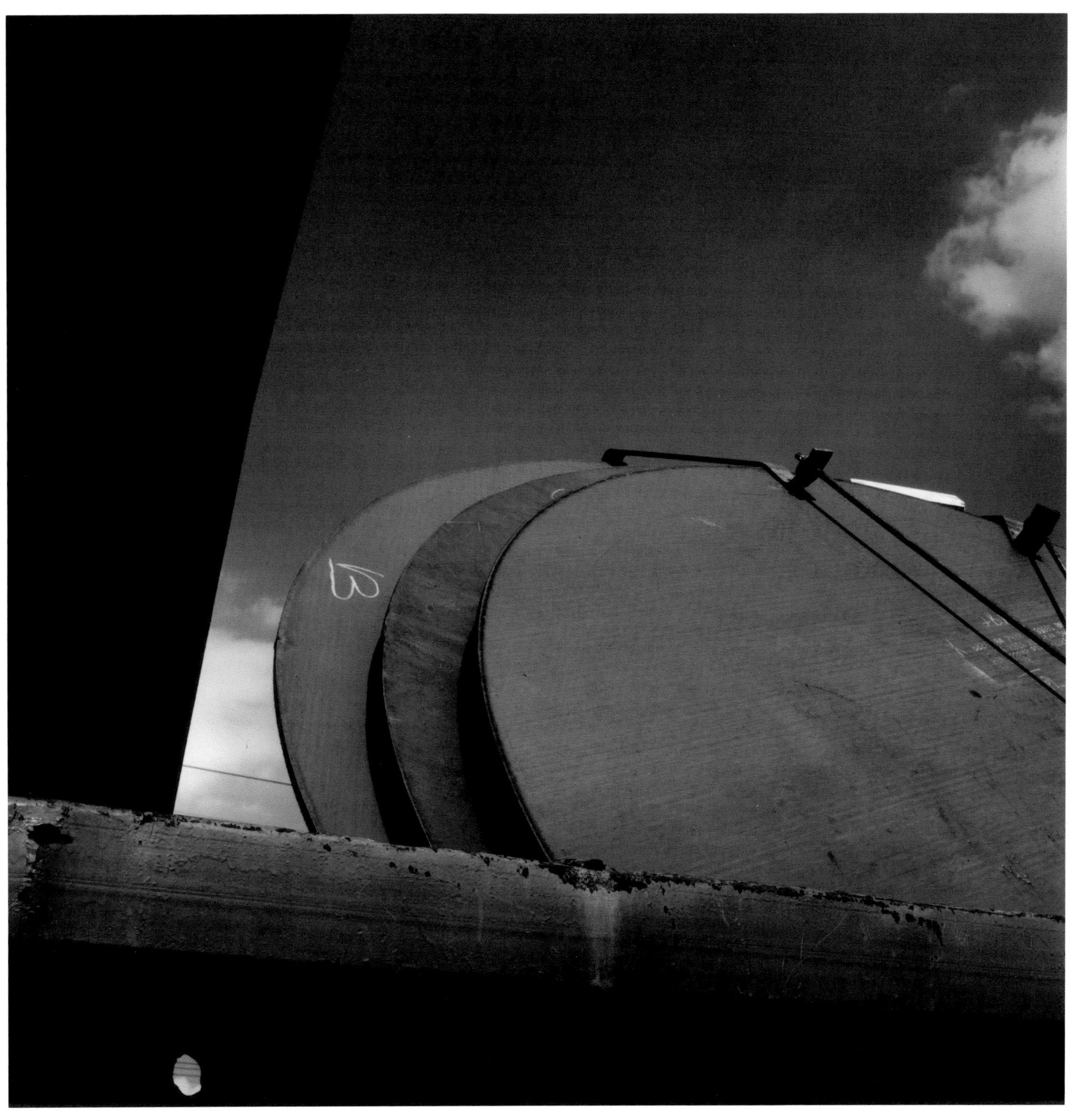

CONTINUOUS HEAT TREATING BUILDING AT COATESVILLE.

ABOVE: FINISHED PLATES LOADED IN RAIL CARS FOR SHIPMENT FROM COATESVILLE.

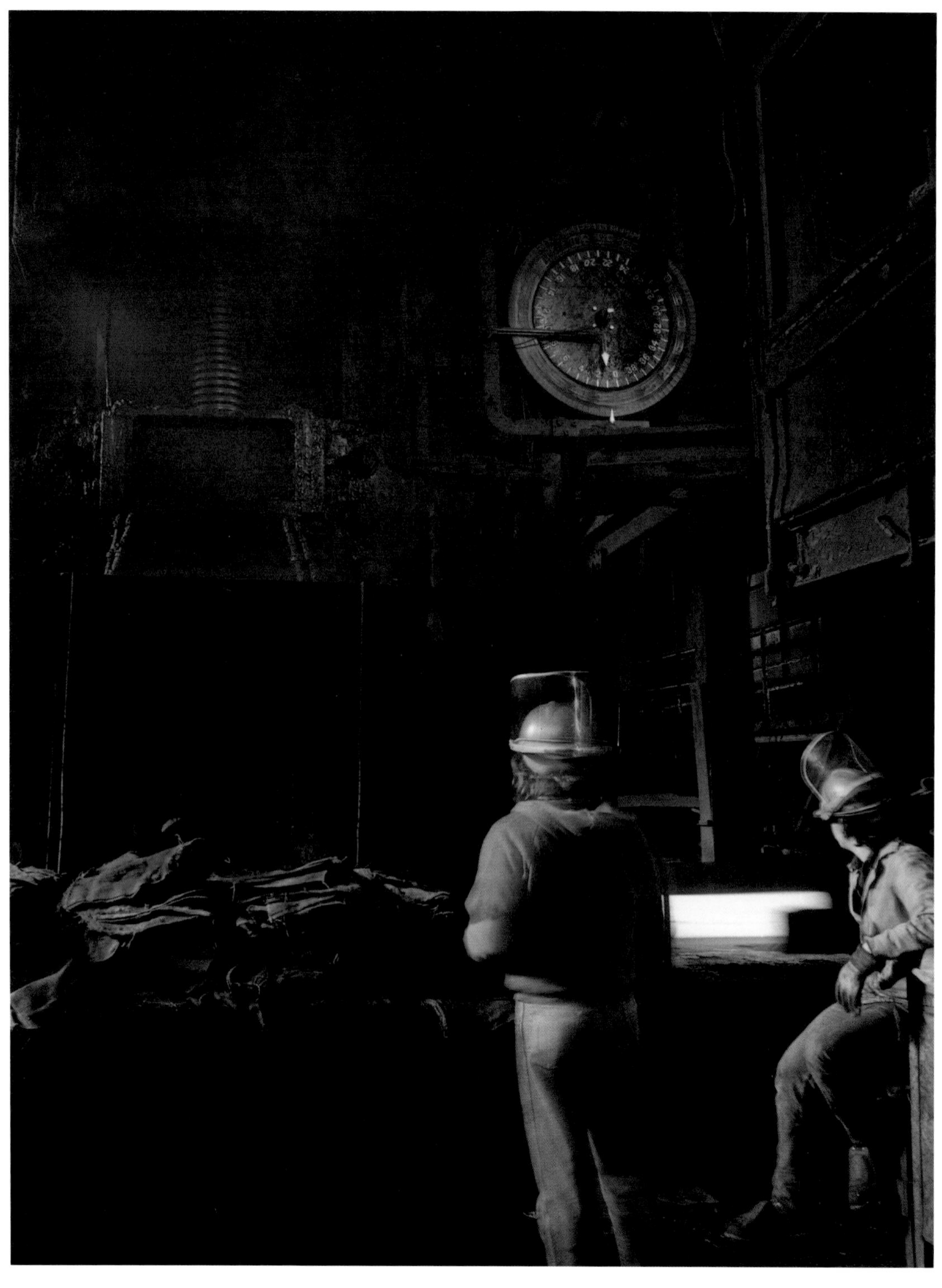

THE SEVENTY-TWO YEAR
OLD 206-INCH
MILL AT COATESVILLE.

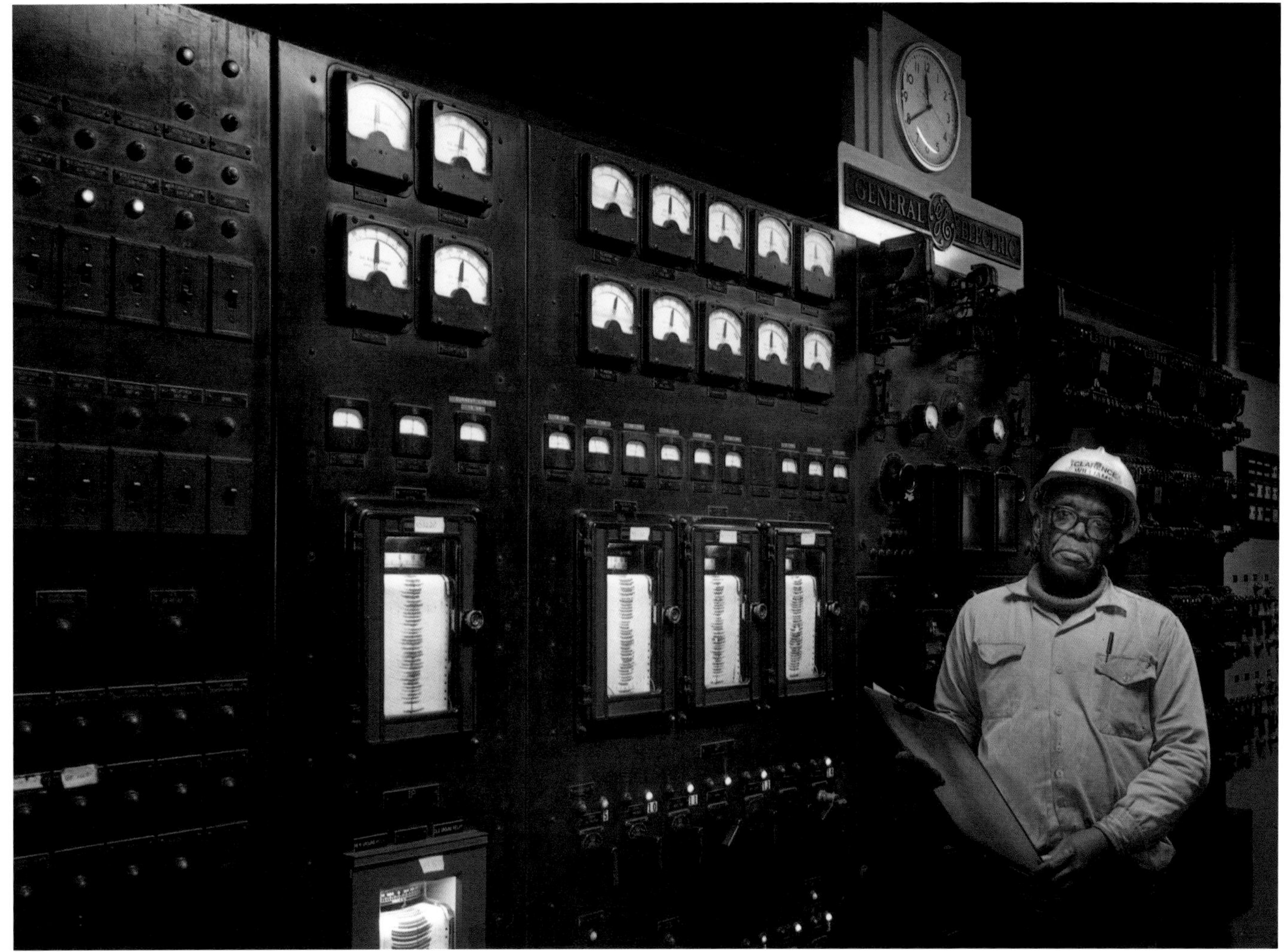

CLARENCE W. WILLIAMS MONITORS THE ELECTRIC DRIVE IN THE 206-INCH MILL MOTOR ROOM.

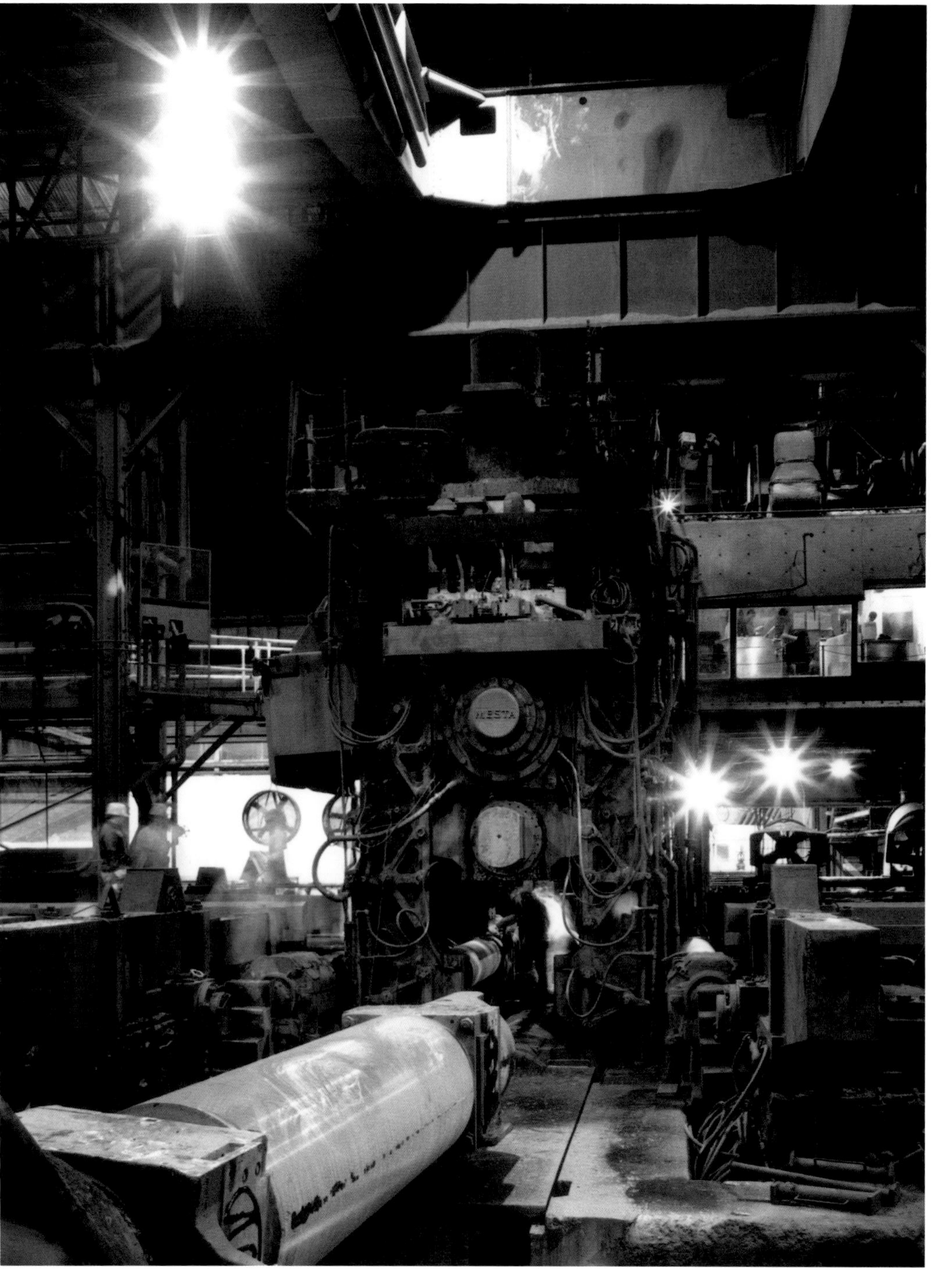

CHANGING THE ROLLS
ON THE 140-INCH
MILL AT COATESVILLE.

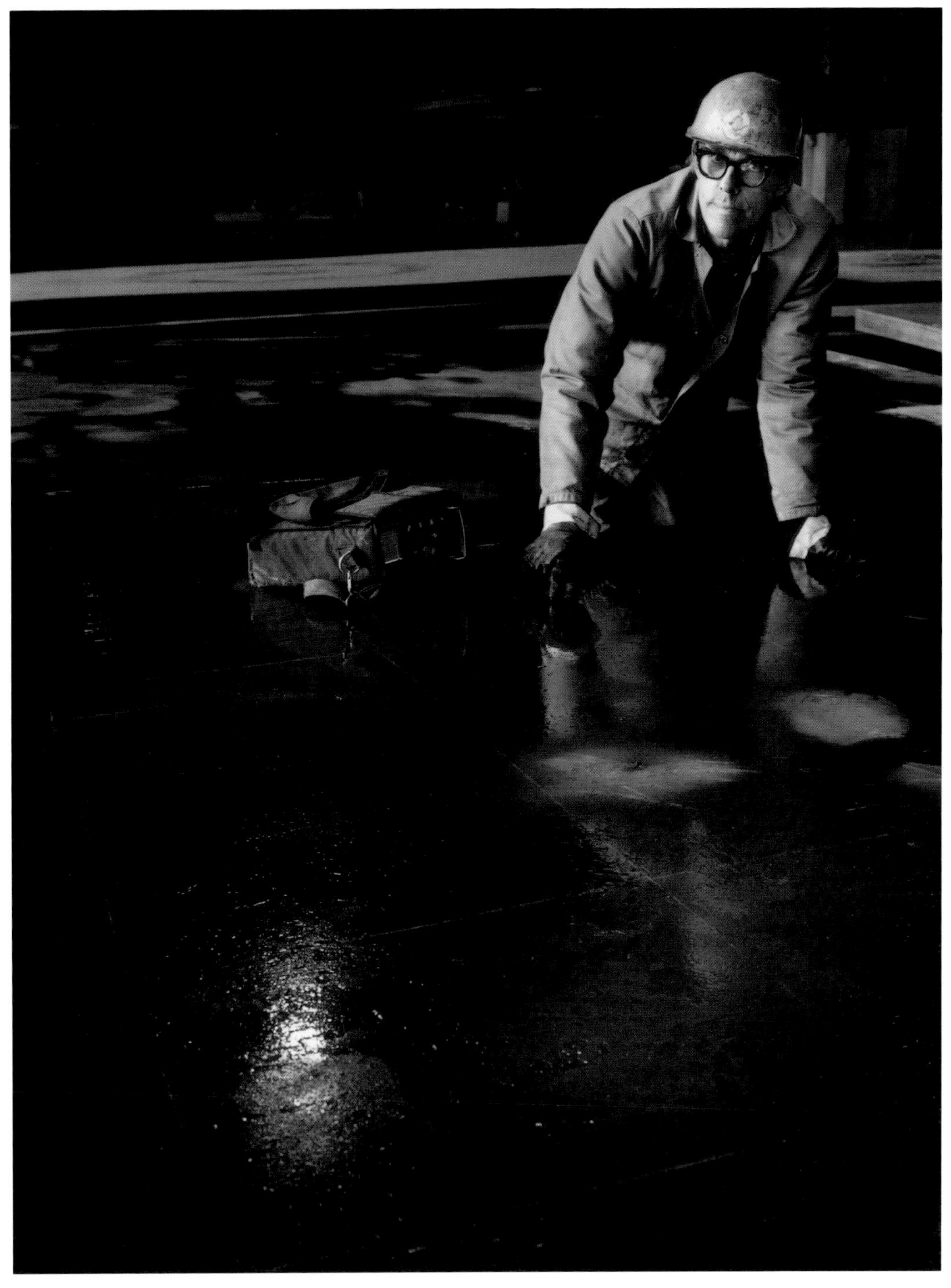

JOSEPH ROMANOSK TESTS ANNEALED PLATES USING AN ULTRASONIC DEVICE.

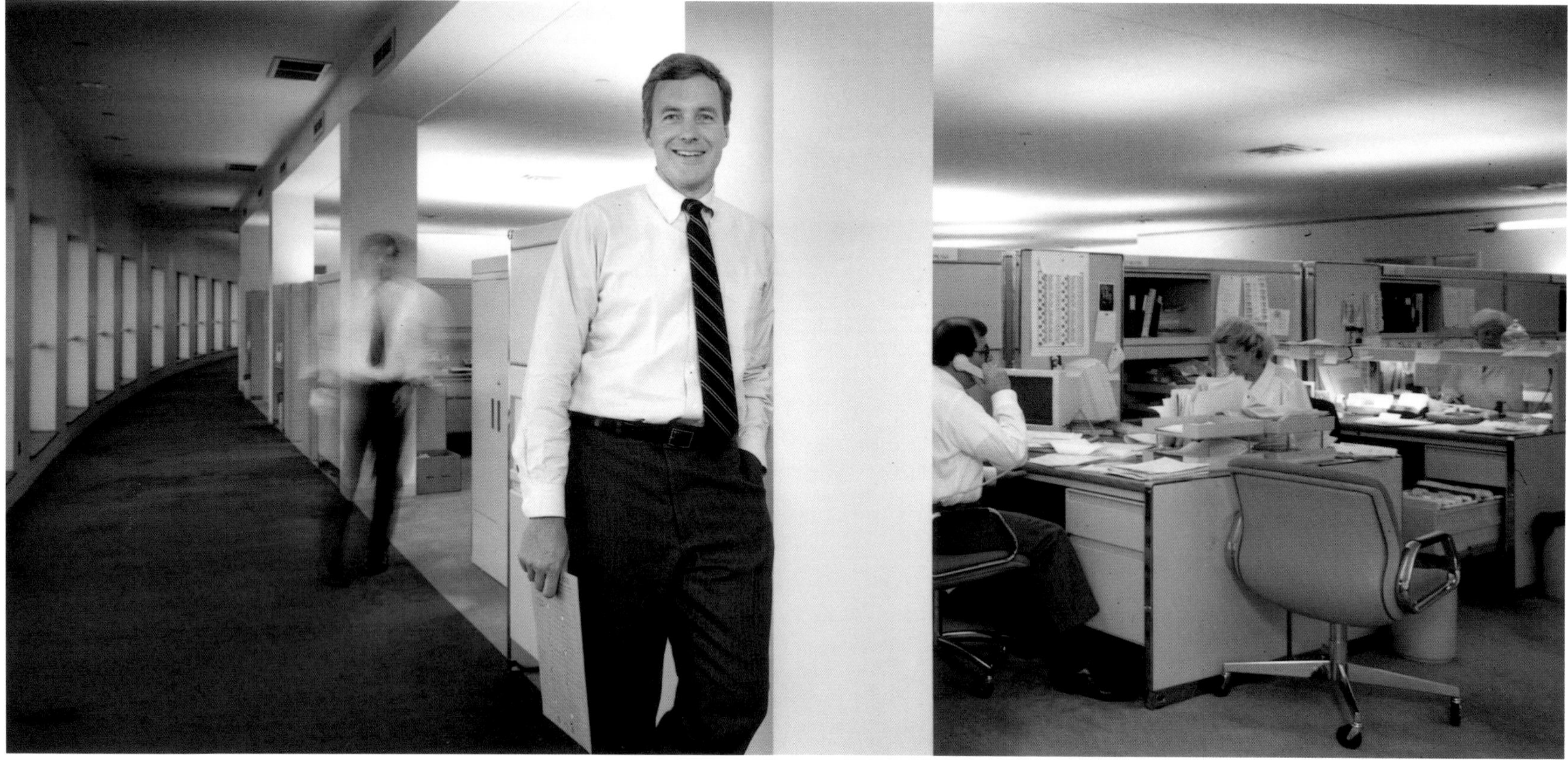

JOE CAMPION, LUKENS SALES AND SERVICE MANAGER IN THE ADMINISTRATIVE RESOURCES CENTER.

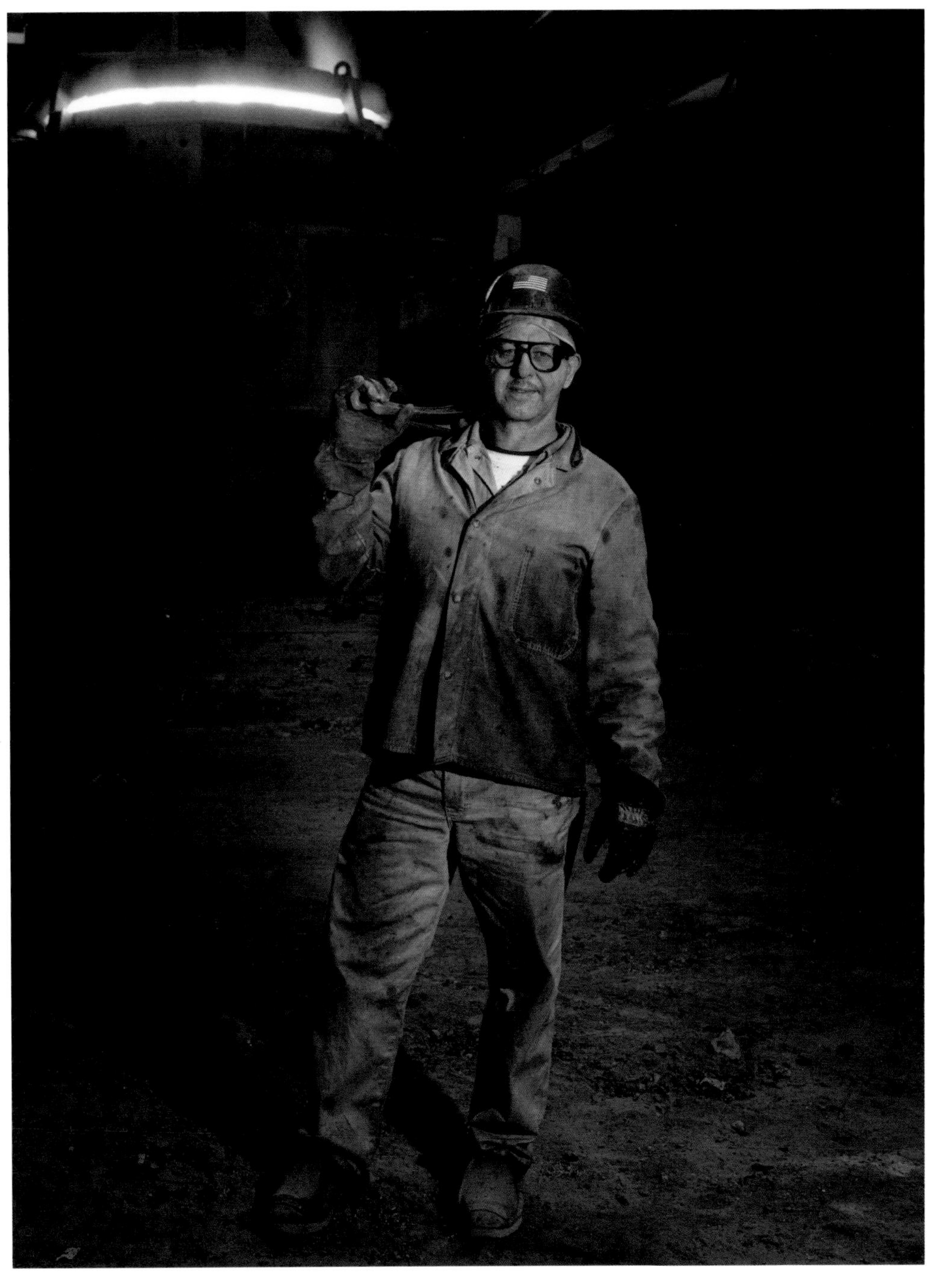

EVAN ALDERMAN,
MAINTENANCE WORKER,
IN FRONT OF A LADLE
PREHEATER IN THE
ELECTRIC MELT SHOP.

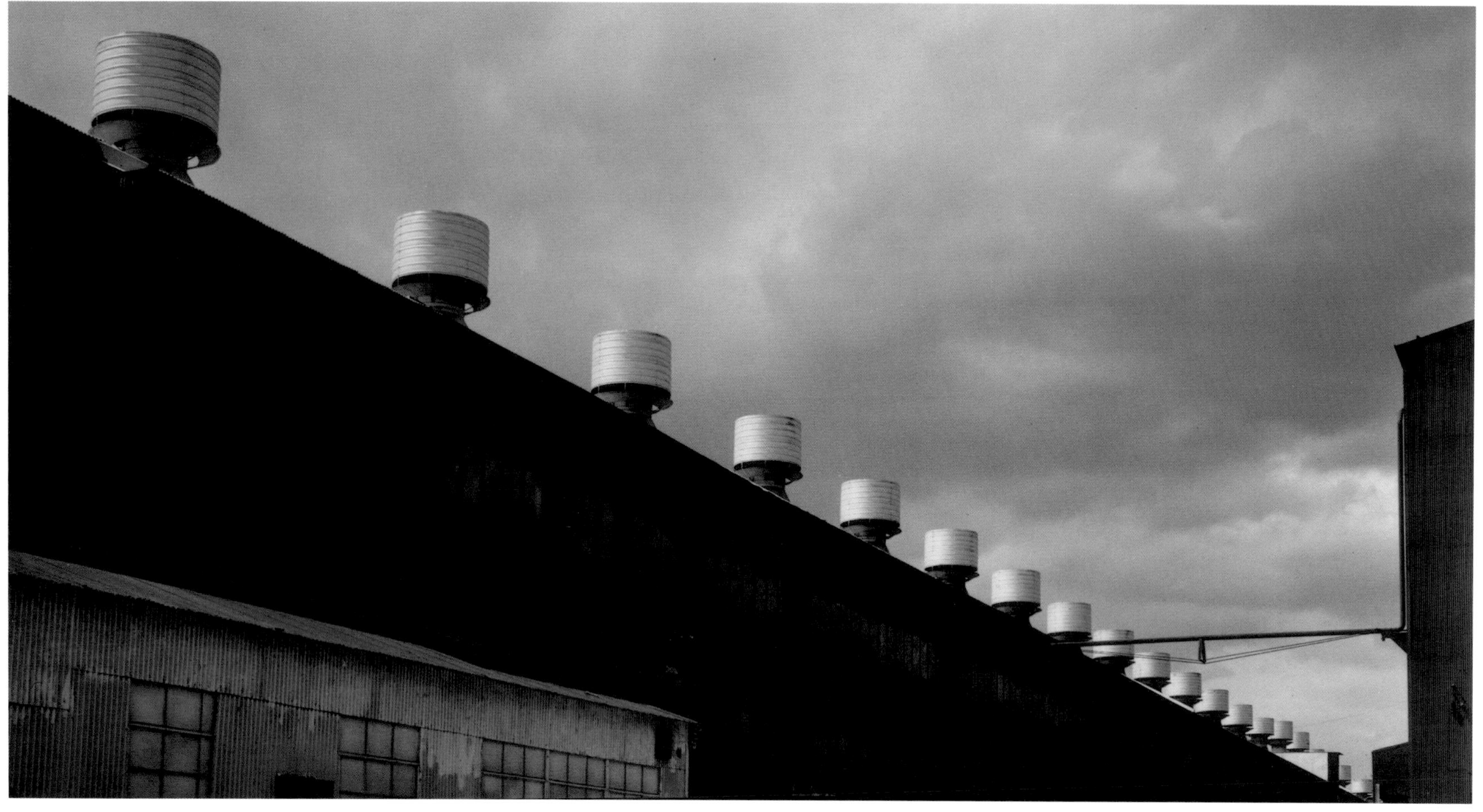

ROOF LINE OF LUKENS STEEL'S CONSHOHOCKEN PLANT.

RIGHT: STACKS FOR THE SOAKING PITS AT THE COATESVILLE PLANT.

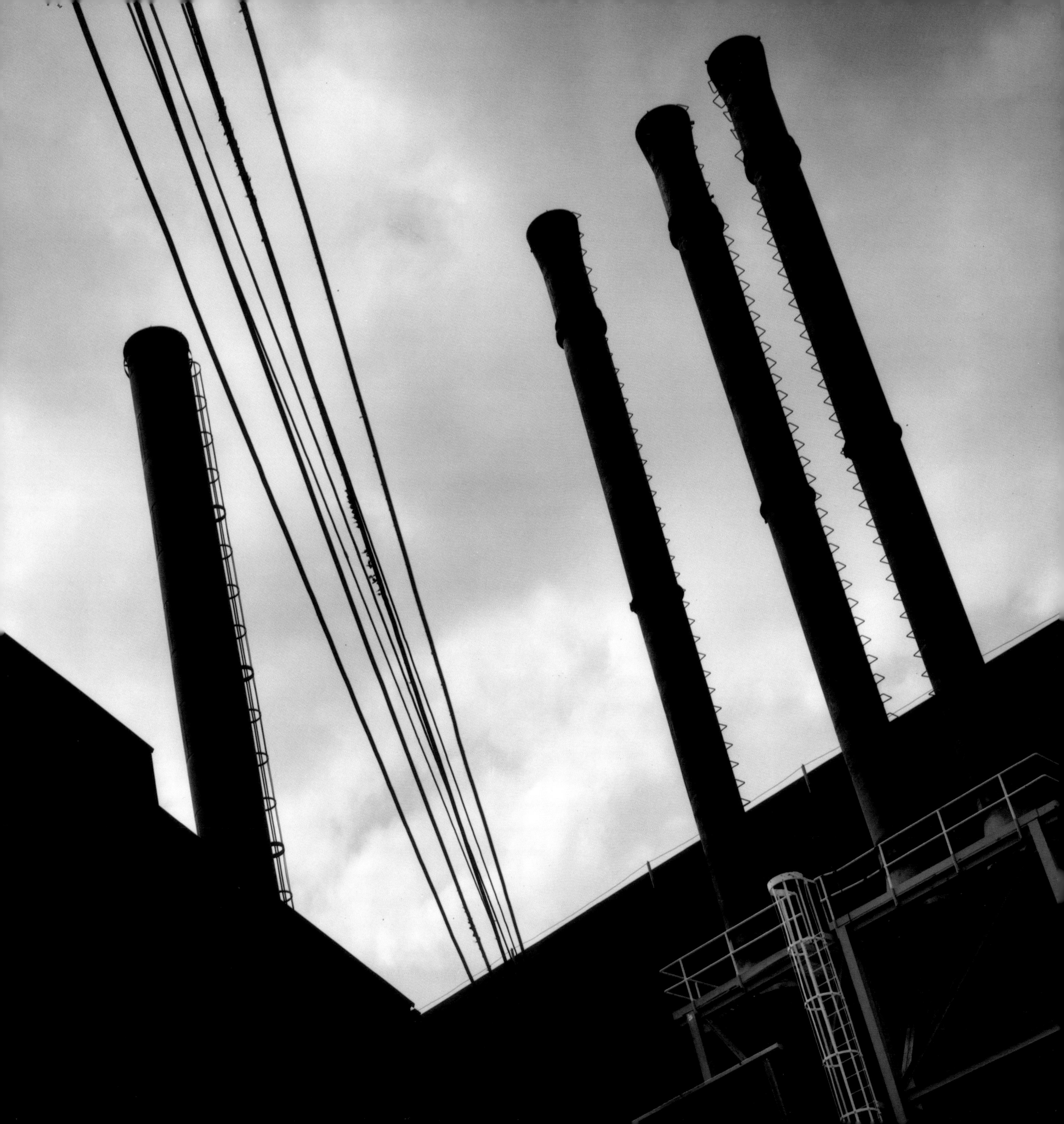

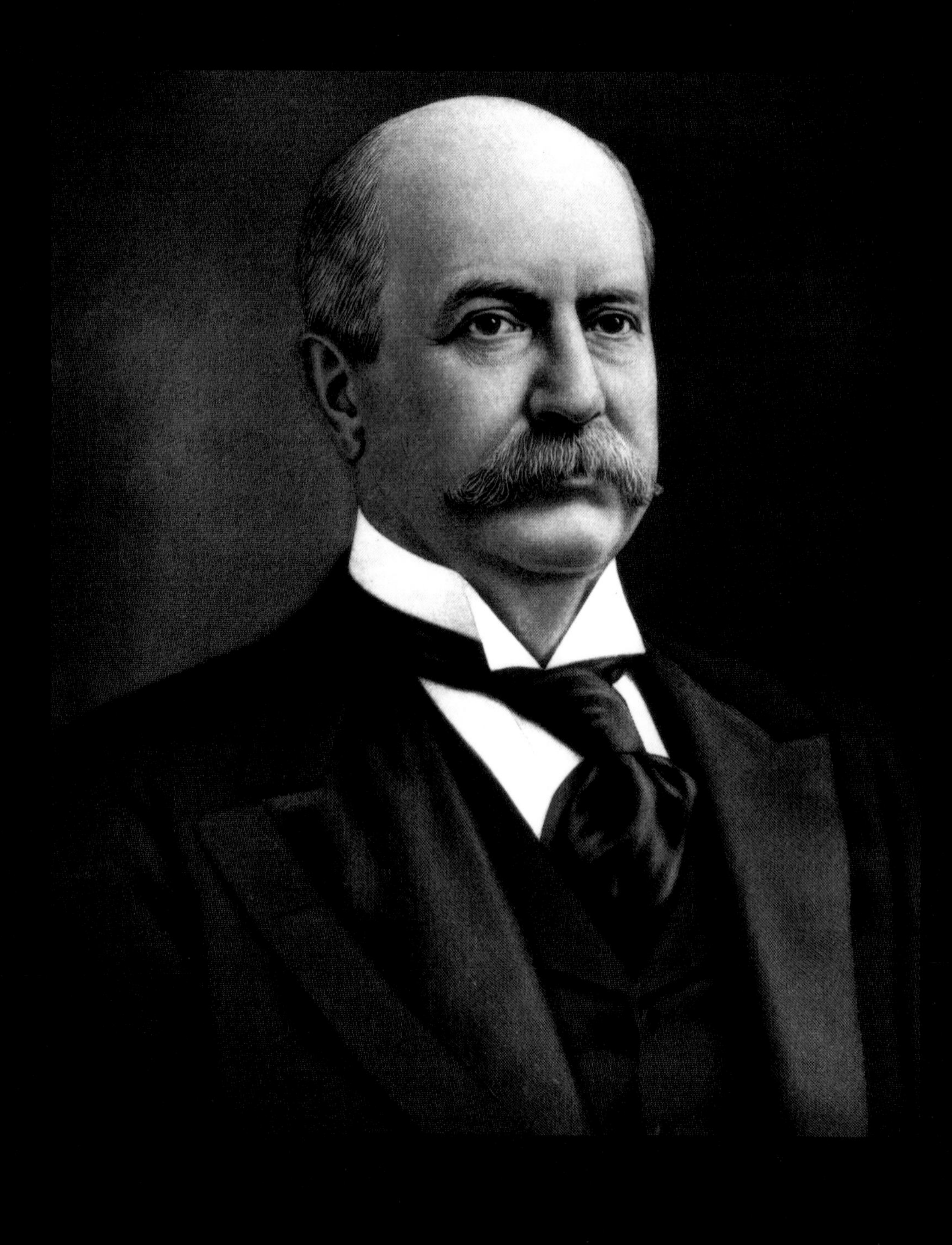

IN THE PUBLIC DOMAIN:

PHILADELPHIA'S TRANSIT SYSTEM

PETER ARRELL BROWN WIDENER (1834-1915), FINANCIER AND EMPIRE BUILDER, WAS LEADER OF THE TRIUMVIRATE THAT UNIFIED AND ELECTRIFIED PHILADELPHIA'S STREET RAILWAYS. HE ALSO HELPED CONSOLIDATE THE CITY'S GAS AND ELECTRIC UTILITIES.

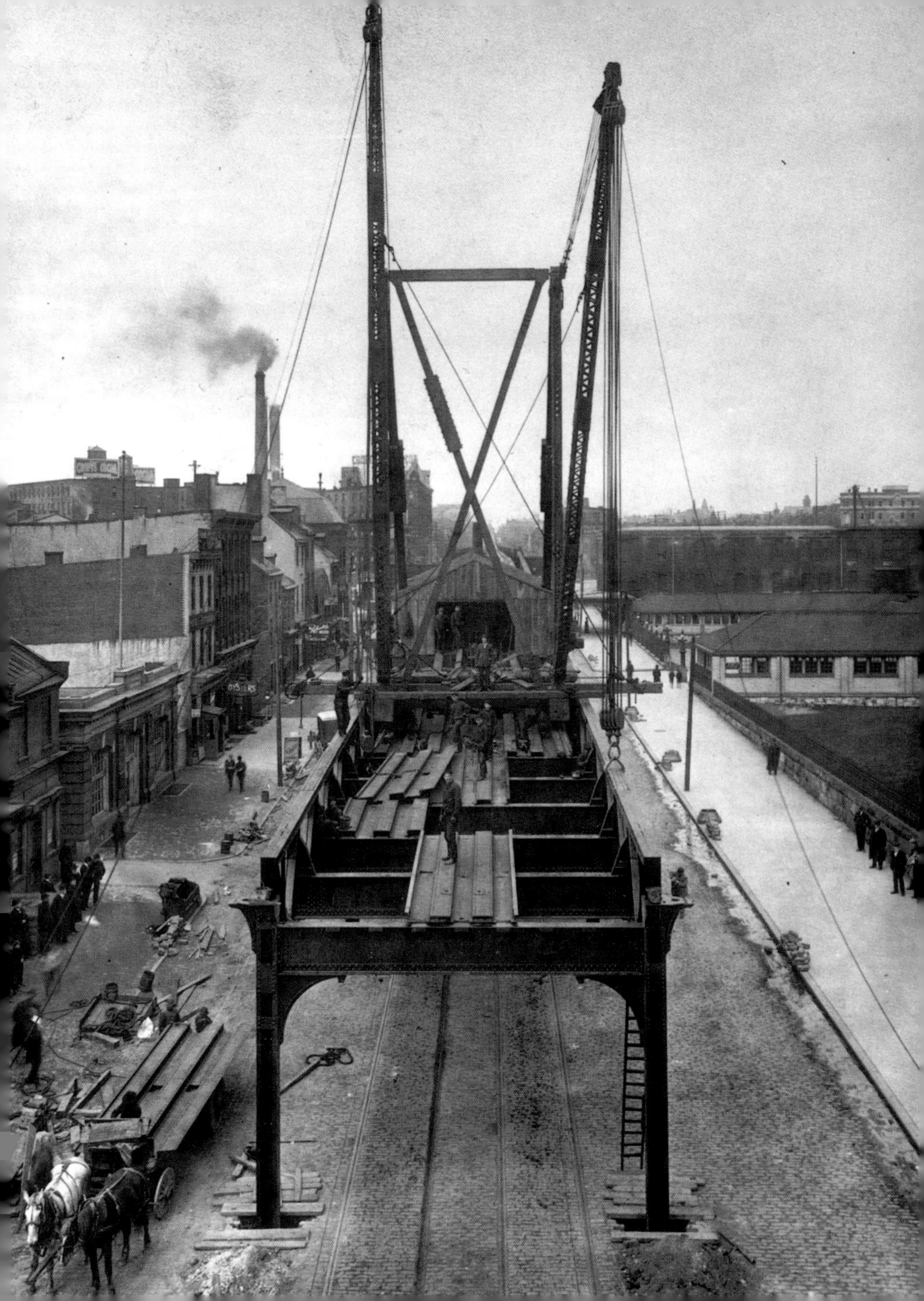
OYSTERS

In the early nineteenth century Philadelphia grew rapidly from its original boundaries between Vine and South Streets. When the city annexed all of Philadelphia County in 1854, the only public conveyances were omnibuses, large horse-drawn carriages operating on fixed routes and schedules. Beginning in 1858 private operators began to lay tracks for horse-drawn street cars, and by 1876 there were nineteen companies operating 289 miles of track and carrying 117 million passengers annually.

At this time, only white-collar workers could afford to commute to work on a daily basis. Over half of all trips were made by persons visiting Fairmont Park and other places of amusement and recreation on evenings and weekends or making special shopping trips to Center City. Still, the horse cars facilitated the dispersal of population into blocks of single-family houses in North and South Philadelphia.

Because the horse car lines were private companies operating on the public streets, they occupied a contested domain. Franchises had to be obtained from politicians who demanded payoffs or concessions. The main *quid pro quo* was a regulated low fare, usually five to seven cents. Aside from this sort of crude bargaining, city and state officials neglected or refused to pass laws that would rationalize the formation and operation of streetcar companies.

By the late 1870s the city's continued expansion, the physical limits of animal power, and increasing street congestion created many difficulties for the riding public. With almost no diagonal streets, most passengers were forced to use two or more lines to complete their trips. Centralization and mechanization offered the only solution. The transformation was accomplished by a trio of entrepreneurs, William Kemble, Peter A. B. Widener, and William L. Elkins, of whom Widener was the most optimistic and daring. Each had strong ties to the Republican state and city political machines, and access to capital.

Since the law did not permit mergers, the horse car companies could only be combined by a pyramid of long-term leases. Rival promotors had to be bought out, adding more tiers to the pyramid and more claims on profits. This system brought large returns to the holders of the underlying companies but would work only as long as mechanization could increase efficiency, and population growth in the service area produced a steady increase in the number of riders. Unfortunately, Widener underestimated the costs of mechanization and overestimated the growth potential of the region.

After experiments with cable cars in the 1880s, Widener adopted the electric trolley first developed by Frank Sprague in 1888. The first electric line opened in 1892, and the last horse cars ran in 1897. The changeover cost more than $10 million. Within three years of the creation of the Union Traction Company in 1895, Widener and Elkins had united all the lines in the city into a unified system. Ridership grew by more than 20 percent a year, reaching 500 million in 1900.

Electrification did little to ease street congestion, which could be reduced only by building expensive elevated and subway lines. During a temporary break with Widener in 1901, political boss Matt Quay awarded a series of franchises covering every desirable subway or elevated route to a rival syndicate. Once again, the Widener group was forced to compromise, and the final step of the pyramid was put in place

CONSTRUCTING THE MARKET STREET ELEVATED RAILWAY NEAR 31ST STREET IN APRIL 1906. THE BUILDING AT RIGHT IS THE OLD PENNSYLVANIA RAILROAD WEST PHILADELPHIA STATION. (HISTORICAL SOCIETY OF PENNSYLVANIA)

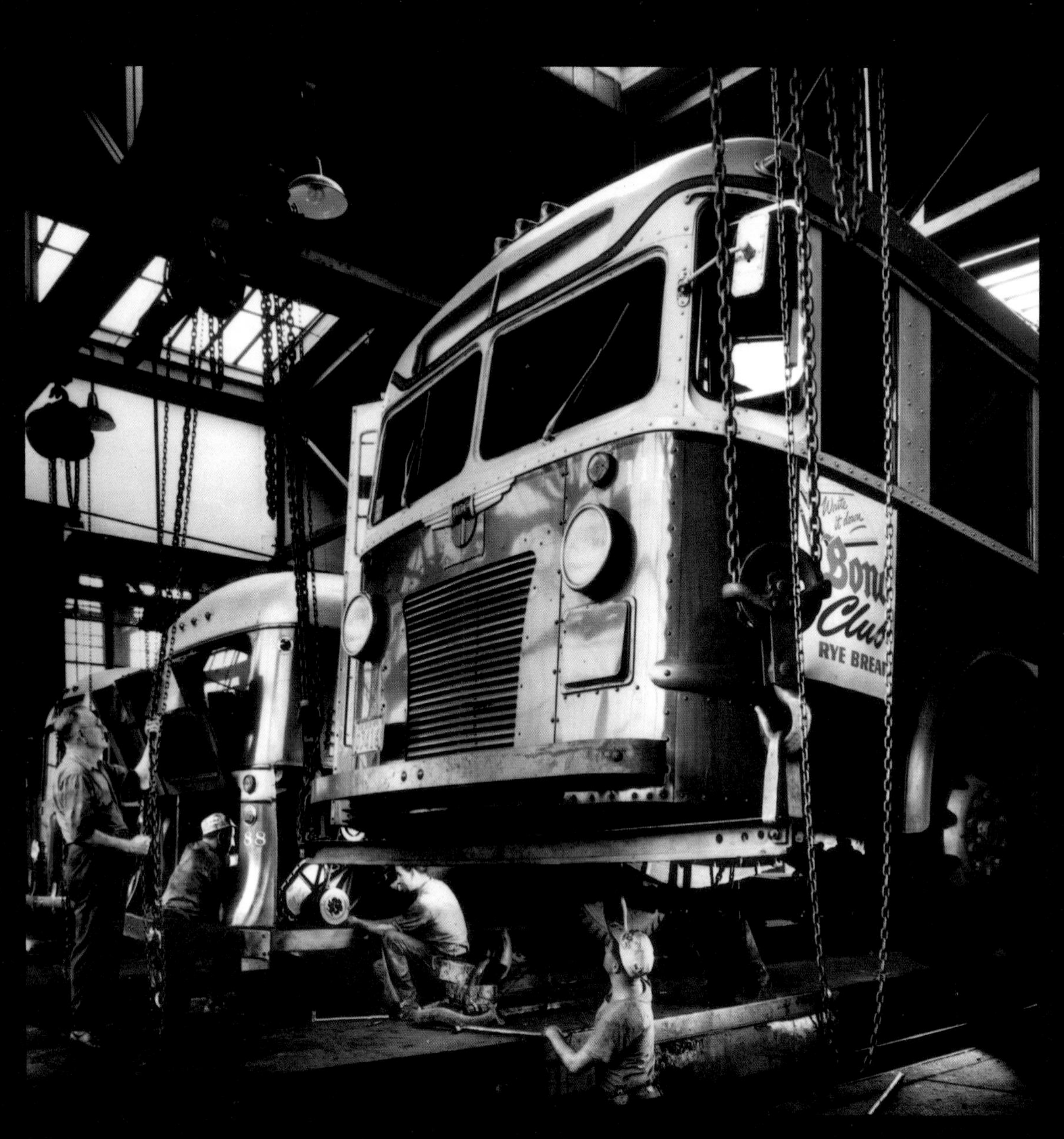
RYE BREA

with the creation of the Philadelphia Rapid Transit Company in 1902. The Market Street subway and elevated opened between 15th and 69th Streets in March 1907.

The cumulative cost of electrification and building the Market Street line nearly bankrupted the PRT. It was forced to defer service and equipment improvements. Its management was viewed as monopolistic and unresponsive and was regularly savaged in the press. With a five-cent fare set by law, wages for streetcar workers were also kept low. Drivers worked on open platforms, exposed to the elements. Discontent flared into disruptive strikes. A municipal reform movement pressed for more regulation. In 1907 the company reached a settlement with the city which permitted the extension of the Market Street line to the Delaware River. The company was relieved of many expensive concessions in return for city representation on the PRT board. Finally, after two long and violent strikes in 1909 and 1910, E. T. Stotesbury of Drexel & Company agreed to refinance PRT, but only if Widener withdrew in favor of a new management.

The new president, Thomas E. Mitten, an up-from-the-ranks operating man, took over in 1911. In his first years, he appeared to work miracles, buying 1,500 new cars of a modern design and securing labor peace and employee loyalty through wage increases and an innovative system of benefits, profit-sharing, and an employee representation plan. Ridership doubled by 1920, and bus service was added in 1923, forming a fully-integrated transit system. The PRT's bad press gave way to praise, and the Mitten Plan was widely advertised as a formula for prosperity and industrial democracy. It was at this time also that streetcar and subway commuting became practical for blue-collar workers. Large establishments like the Hog Island Shipyard were dependent on the trolleys.

In 1912 reformers created a Department of City Transit, which, while often at odds with Mitten, produced a master plan for a comprehensive system of subways and elevateds to be built by the city and leased to PRT for operation. The first of these, the extension of the Market Street line to Frankford, opened in 1922. The Broad Street Subway between Olney and City Hall followed in 1928-1932.

Mitten was eventually defeated by the same forces that had frustrated Widener. In 1919 he broke with Stotesbury over the method of raising fares to cover improvements. The Mitten Plan was expensive, and ridership leveled off during the 1920s, forcing Mitten to cast about for new sources of revenue. He purchased the Yellow Cab Company in 1926, started an airline, and tried to take over the Philadelphia Electric Company. Rather than attempt to dismantle the 162-company pyramid, Mitten added several layers of his own, leasing the operation of PRT to his own company, Mitten Management, Inc., in 1924. Mitten died suddenly in 1929, less than a month before the Crash. PRT entered bankruptcy in 1931, and the court appointed a new board and attached Mitten's entire estate for the benefit of the PRT.

Despite their expansive tendencies, Widener and Mitten were kept out of the western suburbs by the presence of A. Merritt Taylor, a real estate lawyer. In 1899 he took over a financially troubled line running from West Philadelphia to West Chester and used it as a vehicle of real estate development. Taylor was quick to exploit the potential of the Market Street

REPAIRING RED ARROW LINES BUSES IN THE MAINTENANCE GARAGE AT LLANERCH, NEAR UPPER DARBY, PENNSYLVANIA, CA. 1940. BY THEN BUSES HAD ACCOUNTED FOR MORE THAN HALF OF THE COMPANY'S REVENUES.

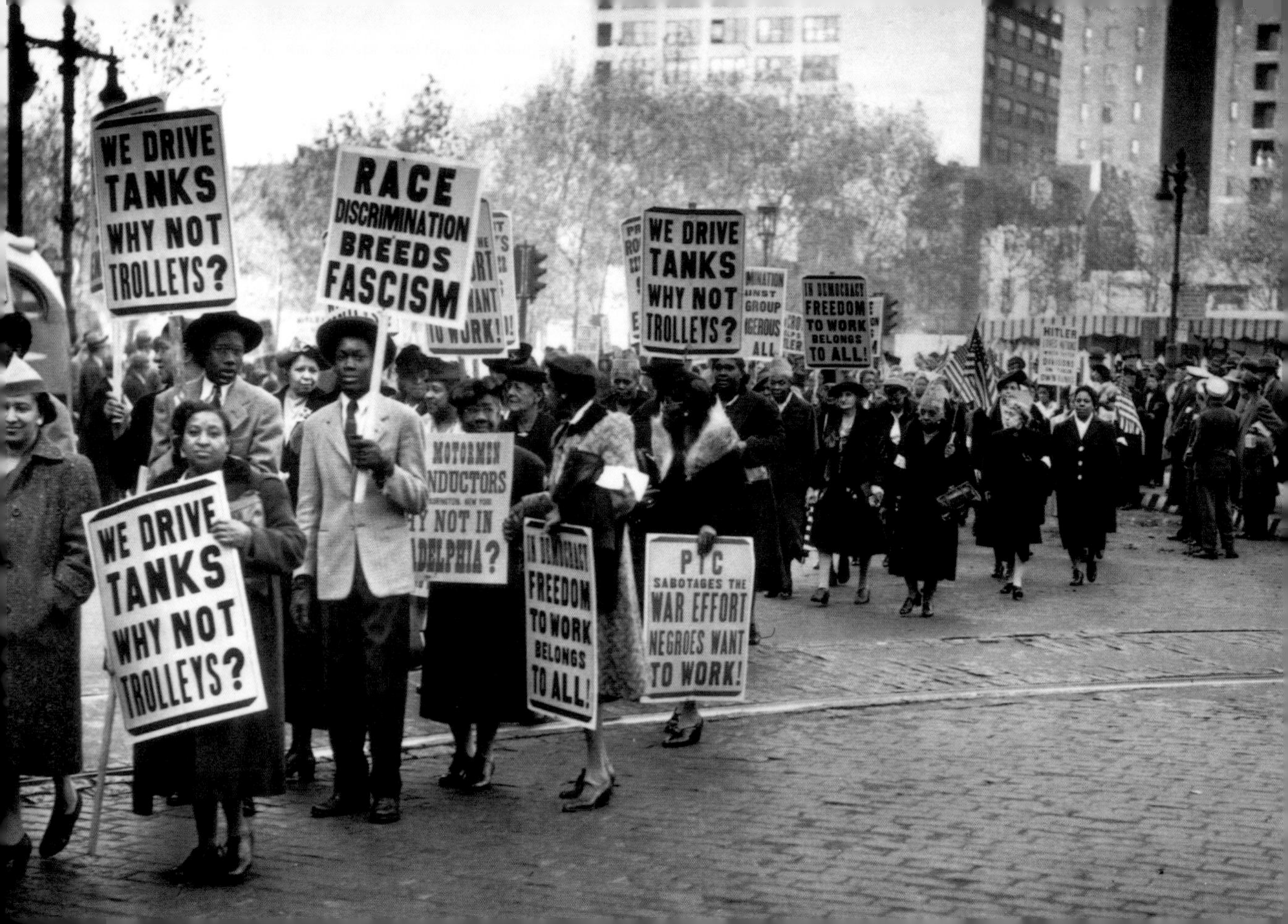
WE DRIVE TANKS WHY NOT TROLLEYS?
RACE DISCRIMINATION BREEDS FASCISM
WE DRIVE TANKS WHY NOT TROLLEYS?
IN DEMOCRACY FREEDOM TO WORK BELONGS TO ALL!
WE DRIVE TANKS WHY NOT TROLLEYS?
MOTORMEN
IN DEMOCRACY FREEDOM TO WORK BELONGS TO ALL!
PTC SABOTAGES THE WAR EFFORT NEGROES WANT TO WORK!

Elevated by developing a network of high-speed trolley lines, mostly on private right-of-way, that fanned out from a combined terminal at 69th Street.

Because it had been built largely in virgin territory, the Taylor system, popularly known as the Red Arrow Lines, escaped the political logrolling and the financial pyramiding of the PRT. Red Arrow was a prosperous family business with a small workforce and a paternalistic system of labor relations that kept it free of strikes until 1963.

The new PRT management made some headway in simplifying the pyramid, and the firm emerged from reorganization as the Philadelphia Transportation Company in 1940. Traffic peaked at 1.1 billion rides in 1943 and remained strong during the late 1940s.

Another major change came in 1944, when wartime labor shortages and protests from the African-American community forced the PTC to integrate its work force. The union local struck, claiming violations of the seniority rule. The army seized the lines for two weeks, and the strike leaders were prosecuted.

In 1954 PTC came under the control of National City Lines, a transit holding company organized by General Motors, Firestone, and the oil companies for the purpose of liquidating urban trolley systems and replacing them with buses. Ridership declined to half of its wartime peak by 1960, as city dwellers bought cars and moved to the new suburbs beyond the reach of transit lines.

A paralyzing strike in 1963 revived interest in public ownership and enabled National City Lines to unload the stripped-down system. On March 1, 1964, Philadelphia, Bucks, Delaware, Chester and Montgomery Counties formed the Southeastern Pennsylvania Transportation Authority (SEPTA), which purchased the PTC lines in 1968 and acquired Red Arrow from the Taylor family in 1970.

The long-standing issue of public control was thus finally resolved. SEPTA has re-equipped and improved most lines, but it struggled for its first quarter-century without a dedicated source of funding. The continuing dispersal of housing and employment further away from Center City has compounded the problem, and SEPTA continues to reach out to the expanding fringe.

AT CITY HALL, PHILADELPHIA, A NOVEMBER 1943 DEMONSTRATION DEMANDED THAT THE TRANSIT UNION CONTRACT BE SET ASIDE SO THAT AFRICAN AMERICANS COULD BE ELIGIBLE FOR JOBS AS MOTORMEN AND CONDUCTORS. (HISTORICAL SOCIETY OF PENNSYLVANIA)

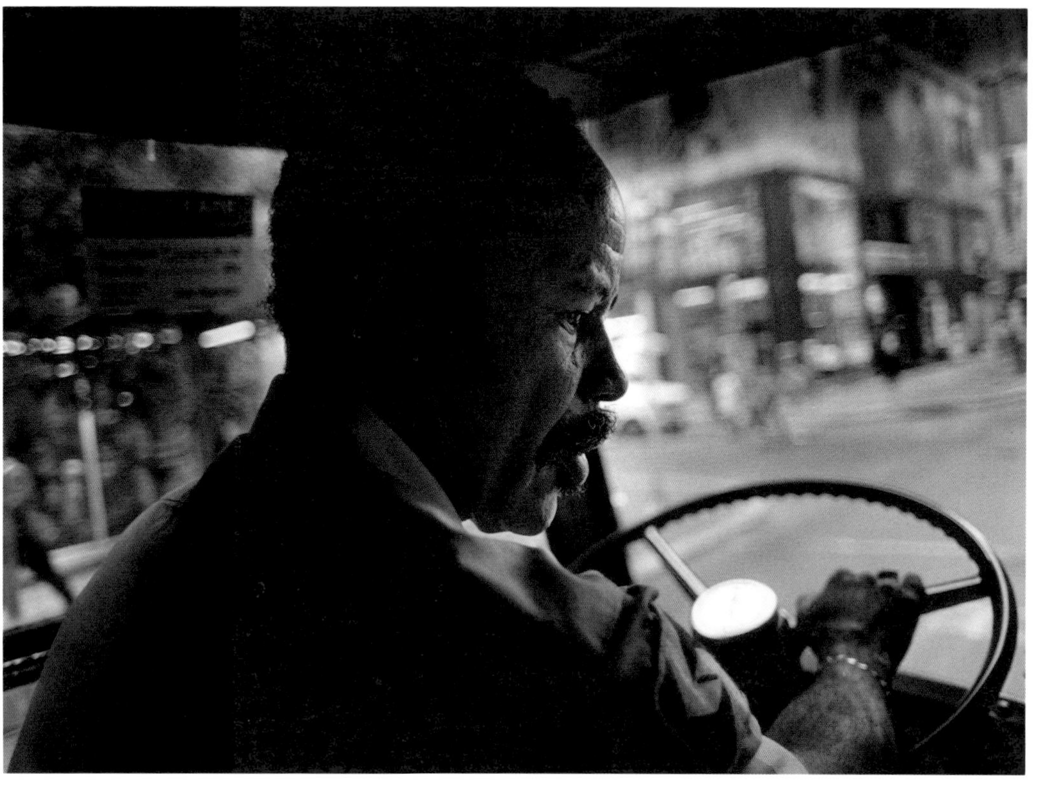

LEROY CHANDLER HAS BEEN A BUS DRIVER FOR EIGHTEEN YEARS.

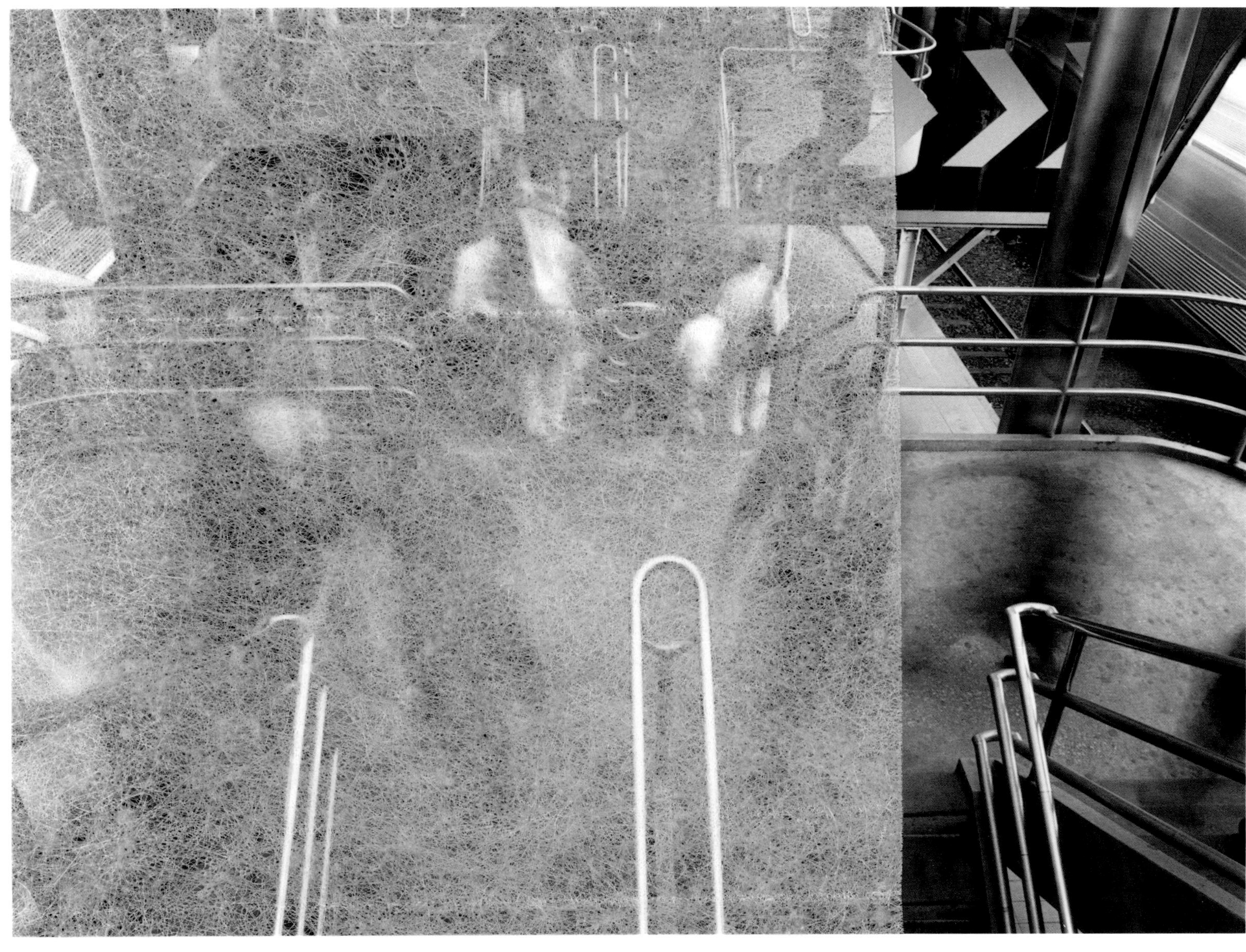

PASSENGERS RUSH TO THE 69TH STREET TERMINAL MARKET/ FRANKFORD PLATFORM.

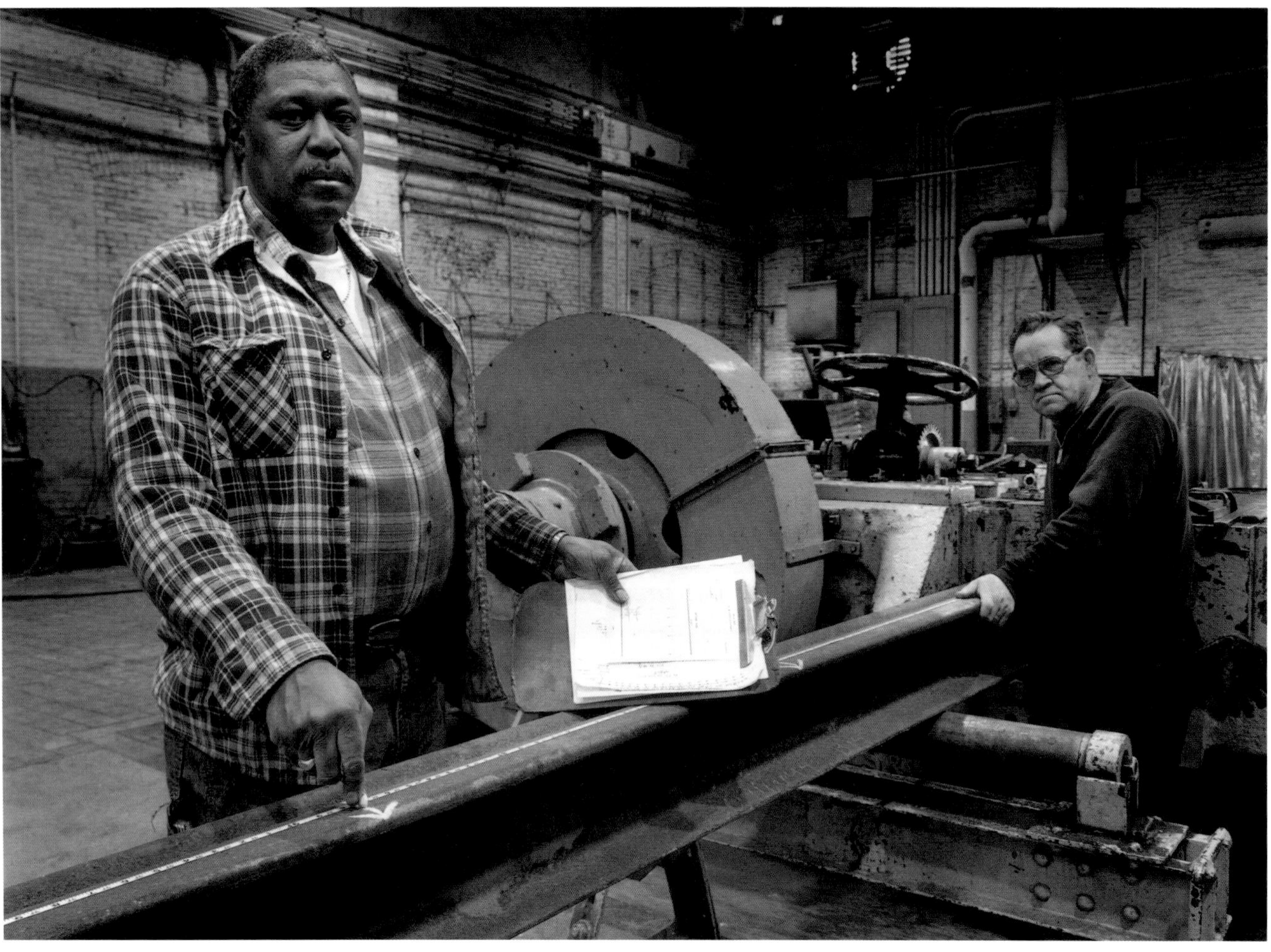

DALLAS JOHNSON
AND JOHN HALL MARK
RAIL FOR BENDING
AT THE COURTLAND
TRACK SHOP.

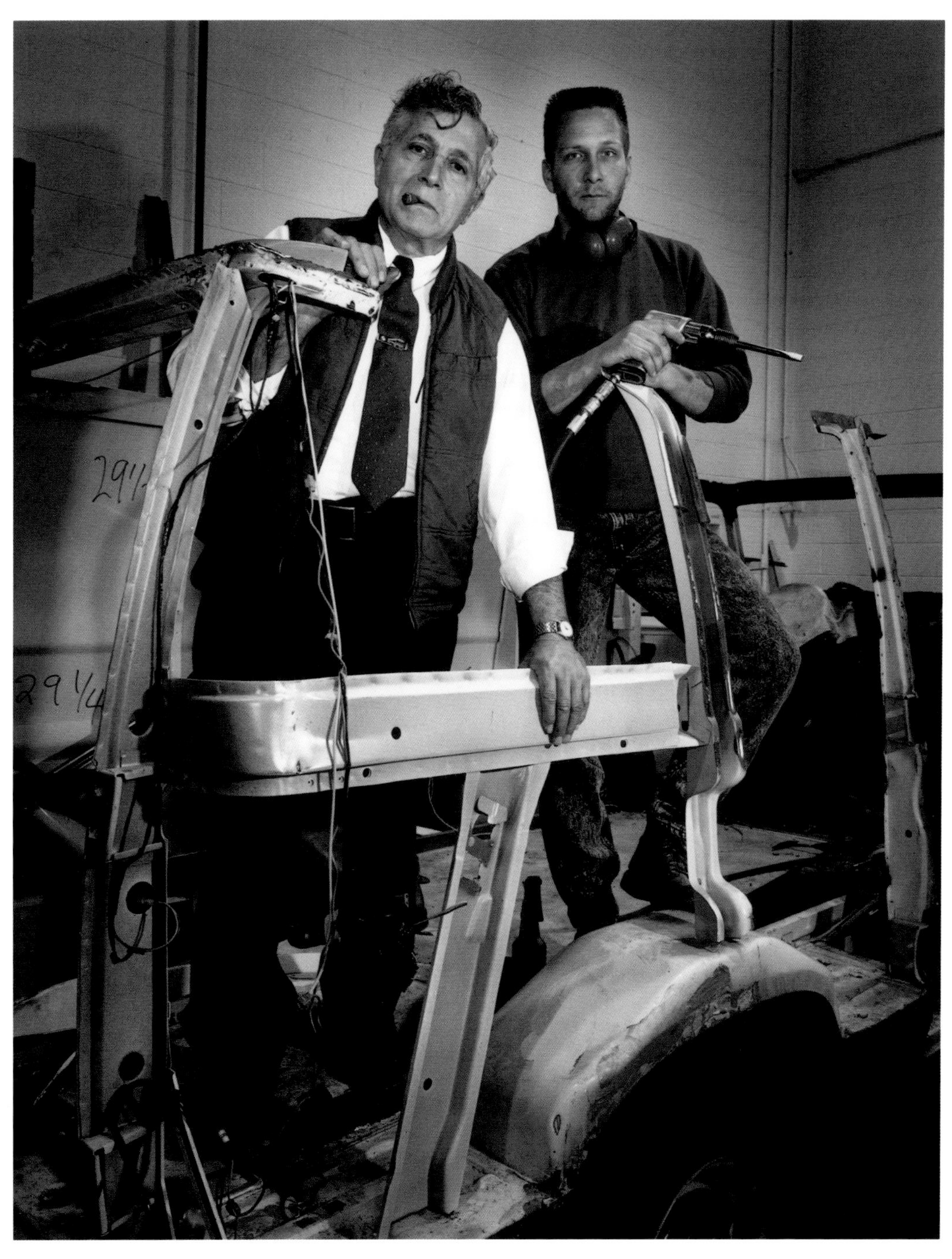

DOMINIC DISANTIS AND TOM HOFFMAN IN THE SECOND AND WYOMING UTILITY VEHICLE SHOP.

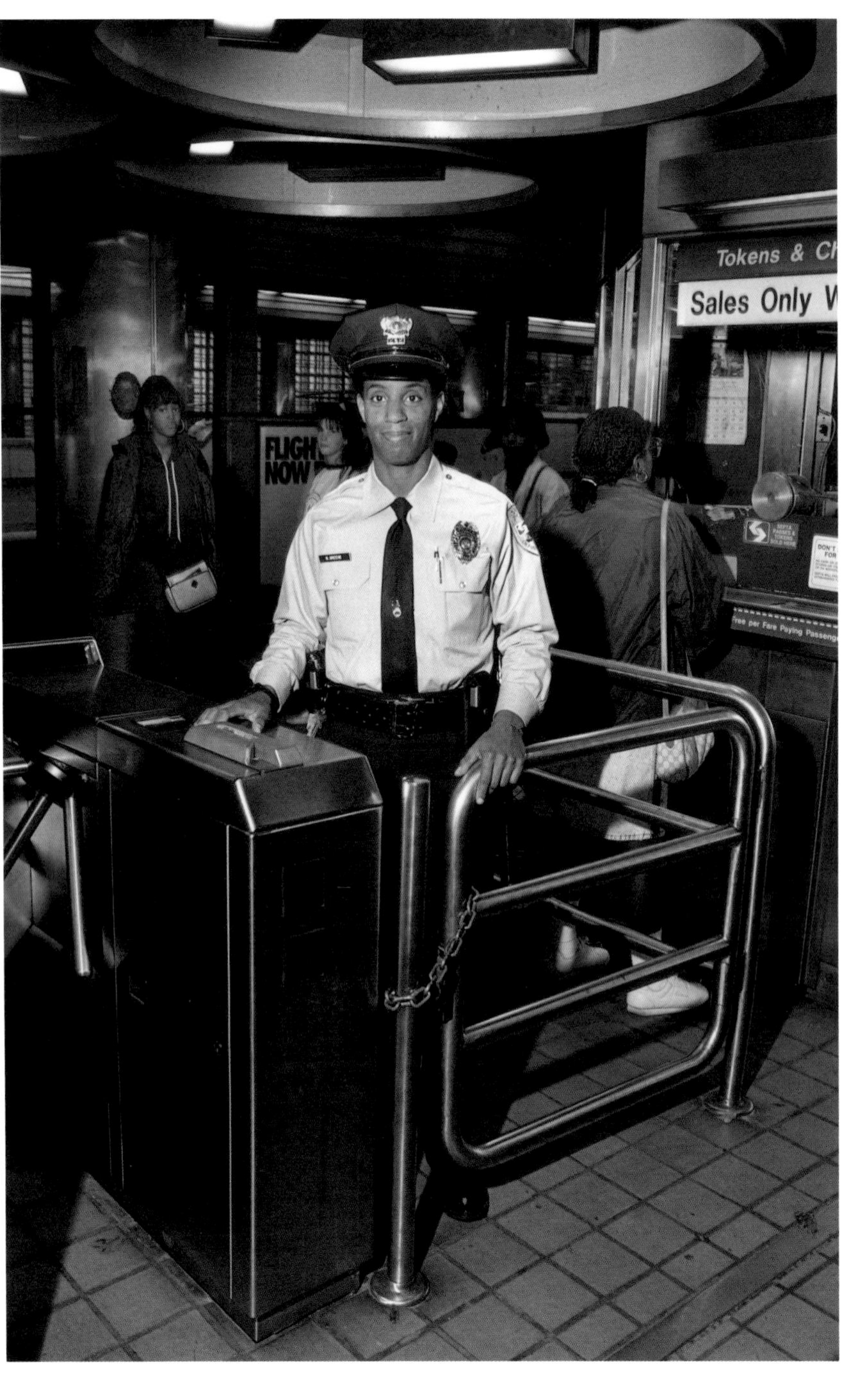

NATALIE GREENE, SEPTA POLICE OFFICER, AT THE 11TH AND MARKET SUBWAY STATION.

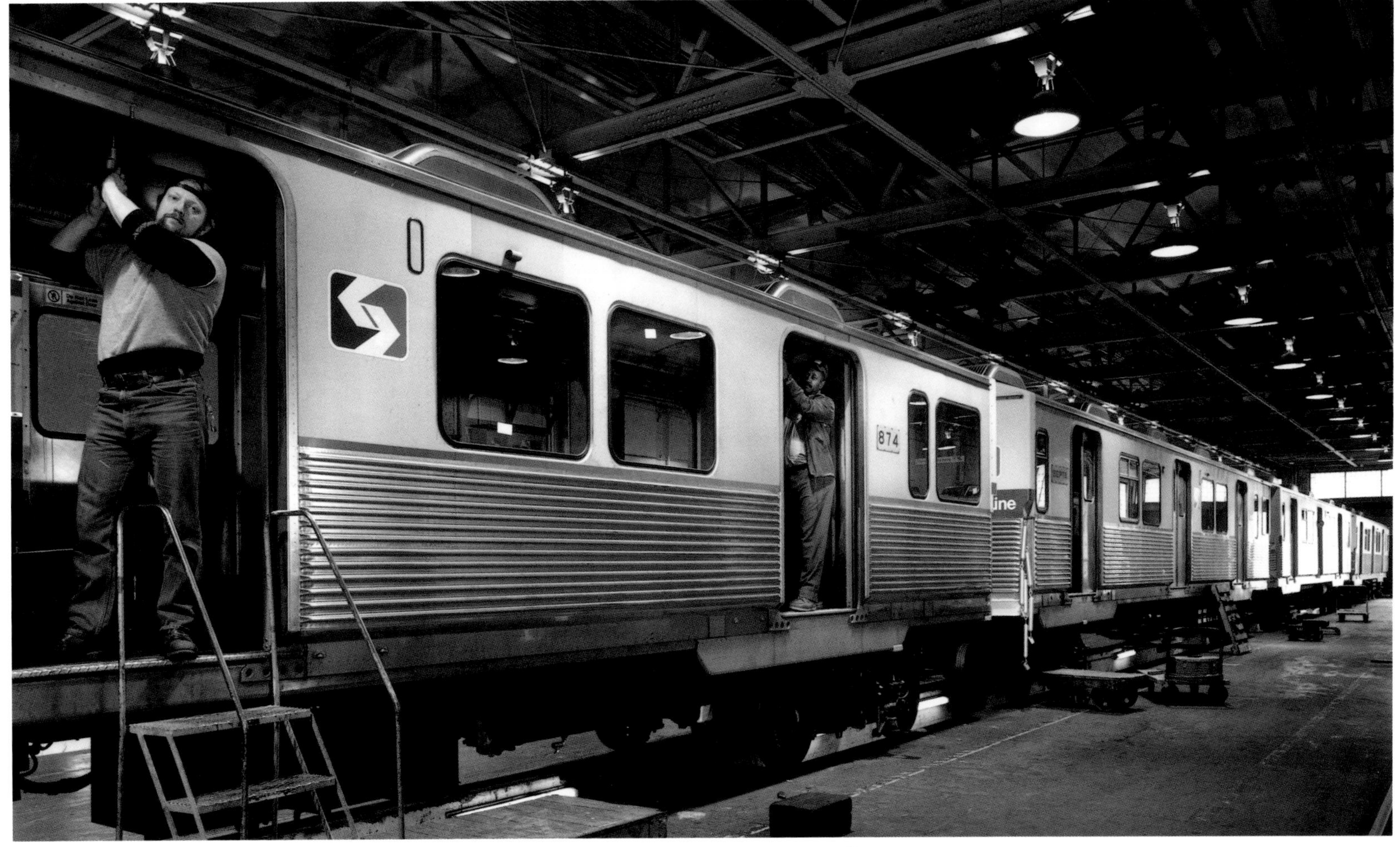

JOHN TAYLOR AND ANDREW STEWART ADJUST ELEVATED CAR DOORS AT THE 69TH STREET SHOPS.

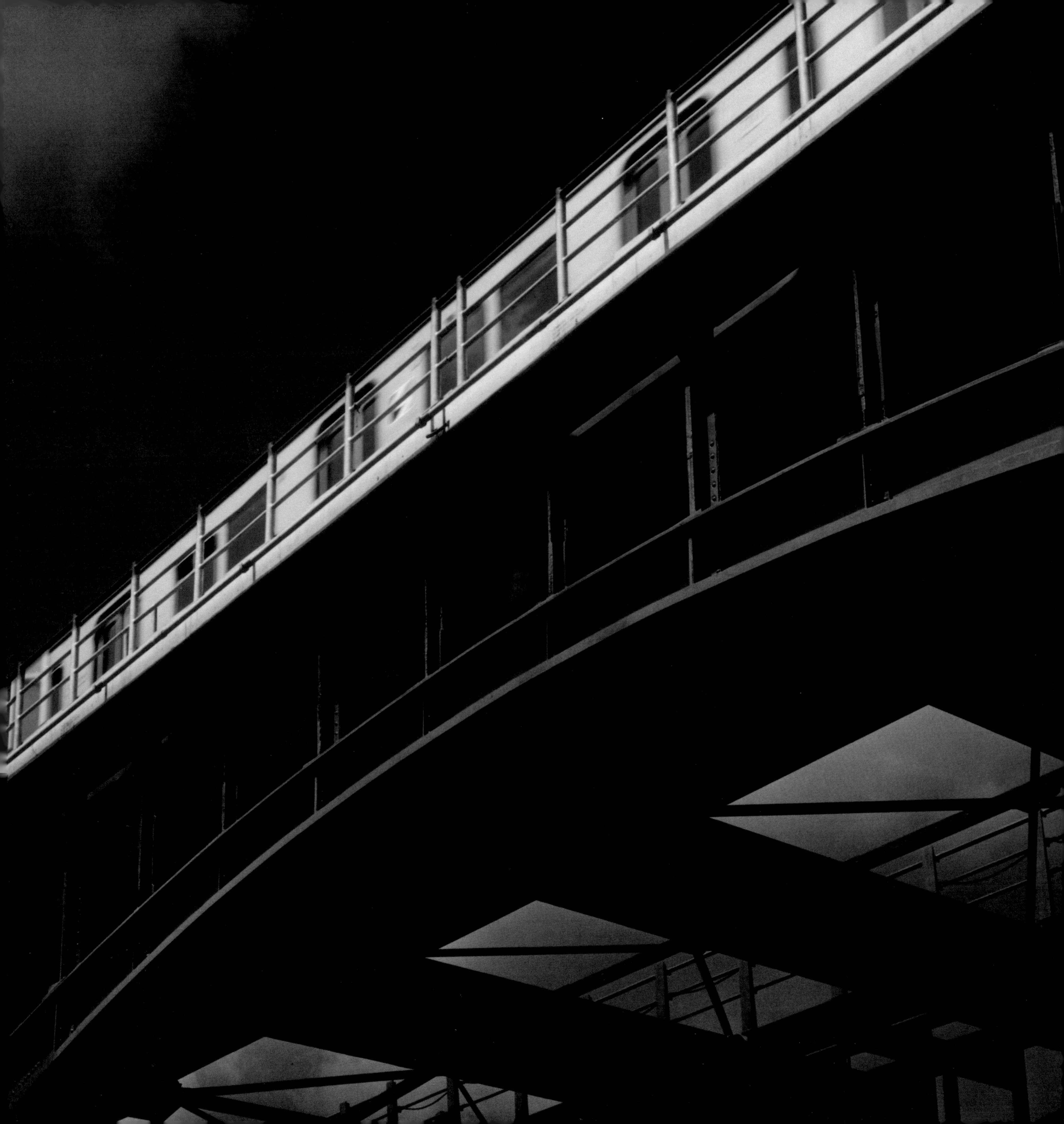

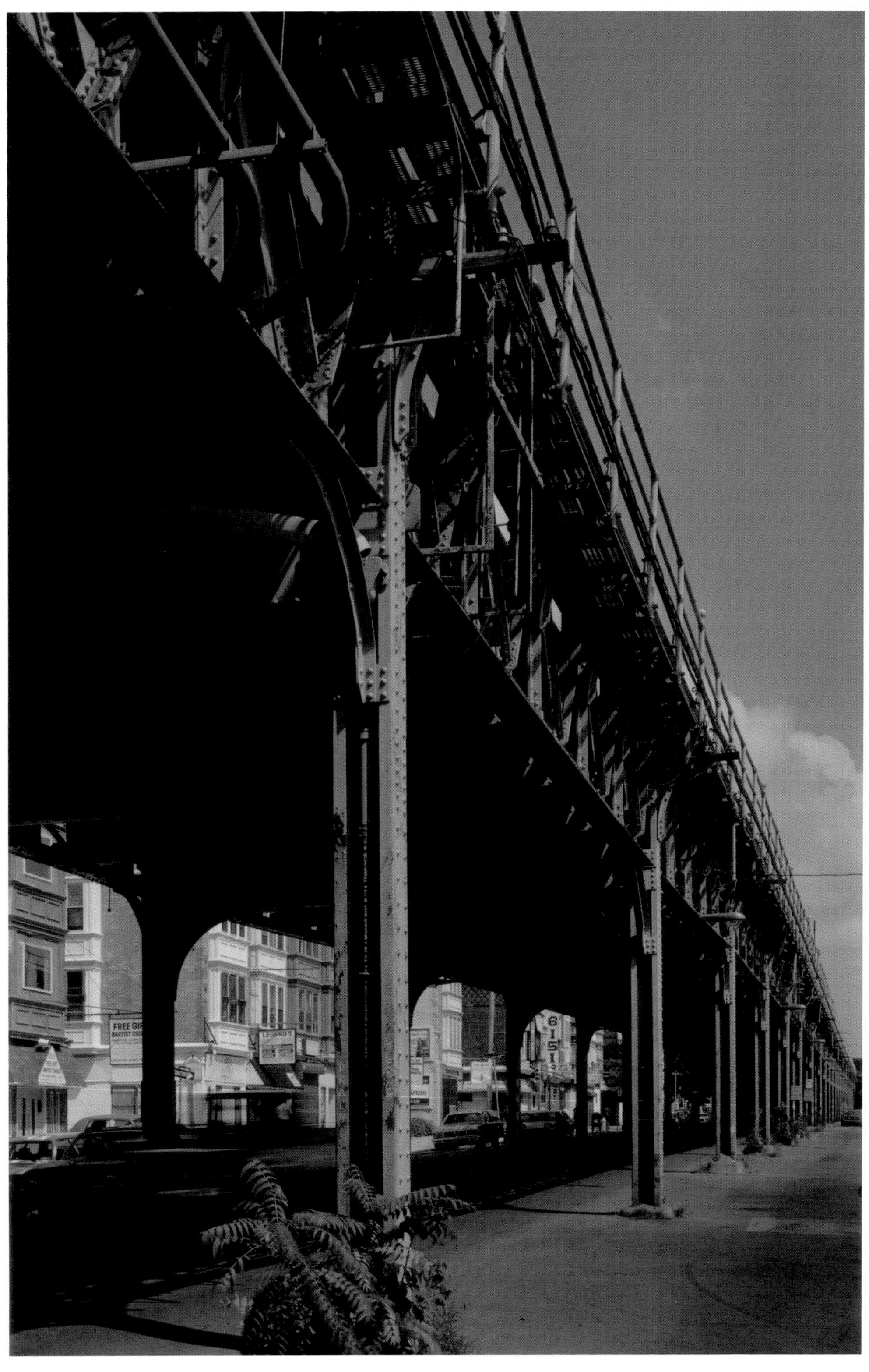

FRANKFORD ELEVATED BRIDGE OVER LEHIGH AVENUE.

ABOVE: MARKET STREET ELEVATED LOOKING EAST FROM 63RD STREET IN WEST PHILADELPHIA.

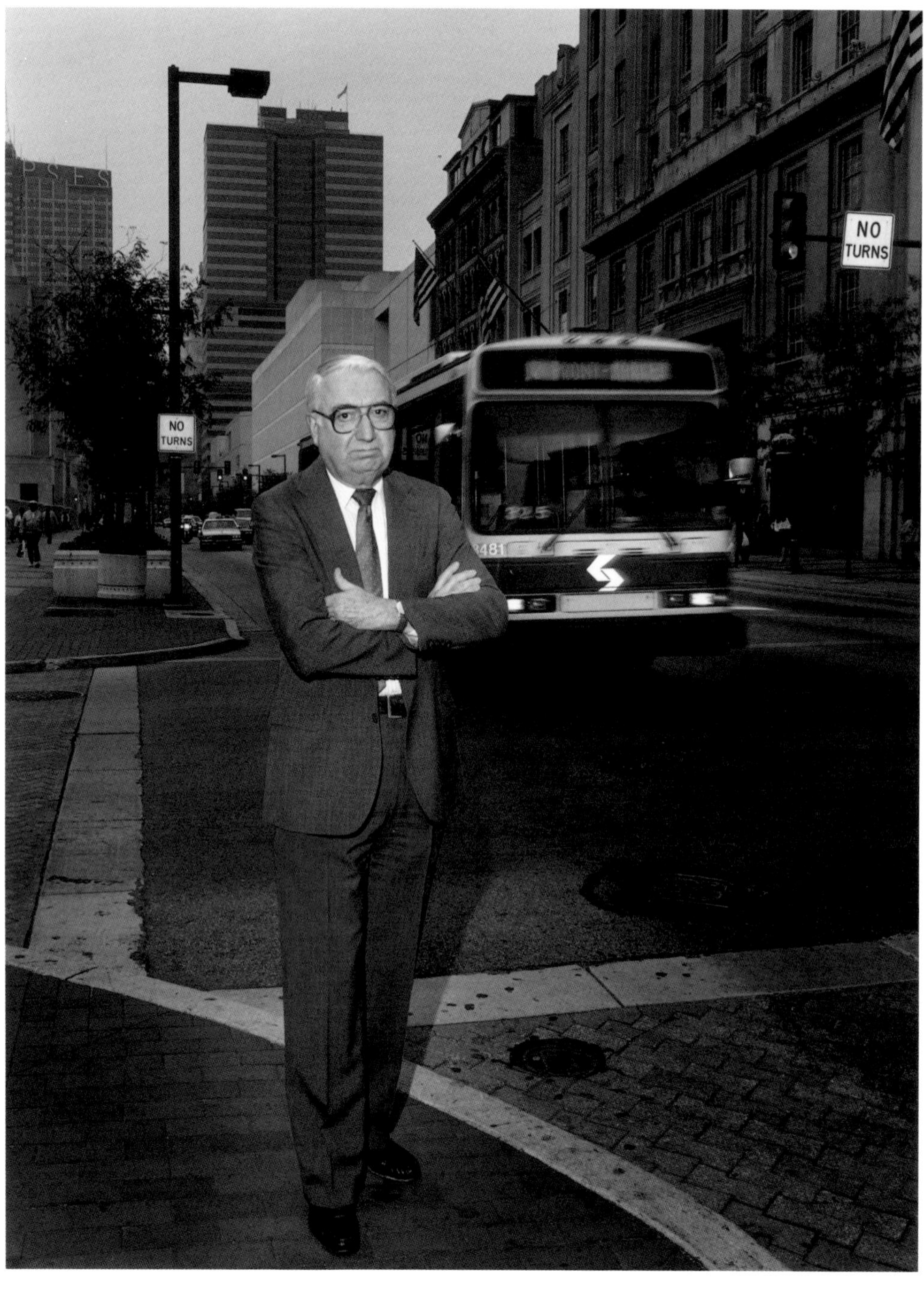

GENERAL MANAGER
LOUIS J. GAMBACCINI
NEAR HIS OFFICE
AT 8TH AND MARKET.

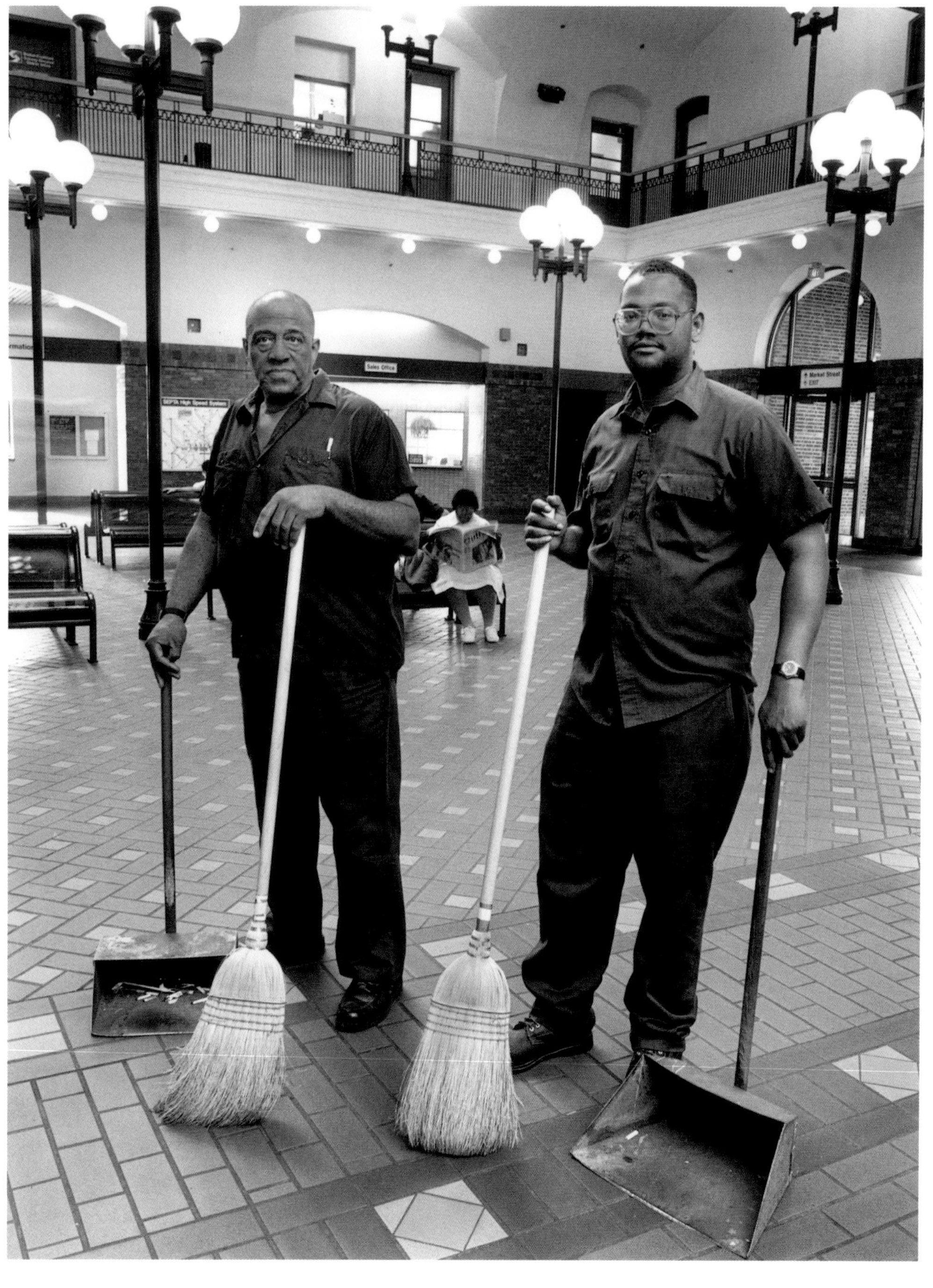

DANIEL YOUNG AND LAMONT CRADLE, MAINTENANCE CUSTODIANS, IN THE 69TH STREET TERMINAL.

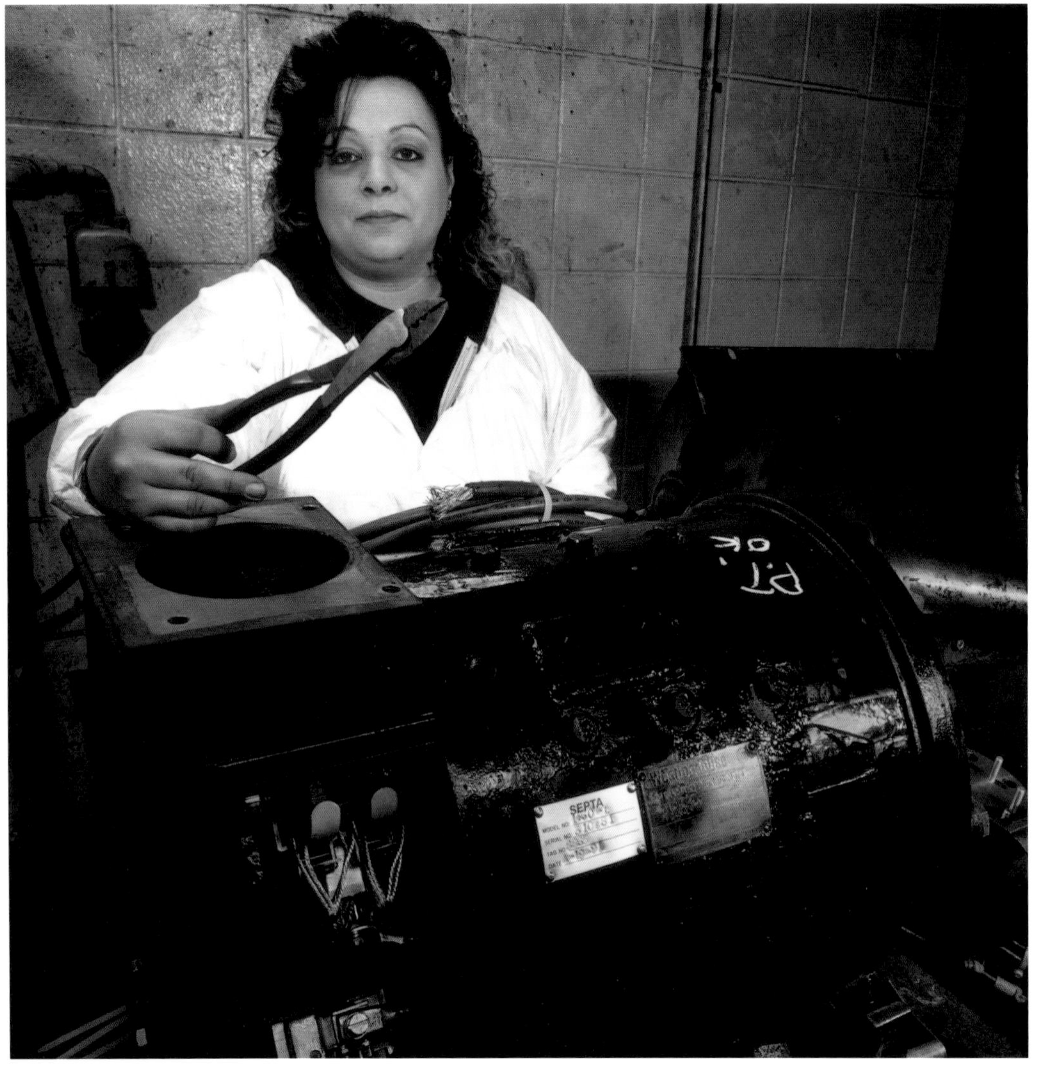

MARIE JENNINGS,
MECHANIC, WORKS IN
A TEST STATION
AT THE 69TH STREET
MOTOR SHOP.

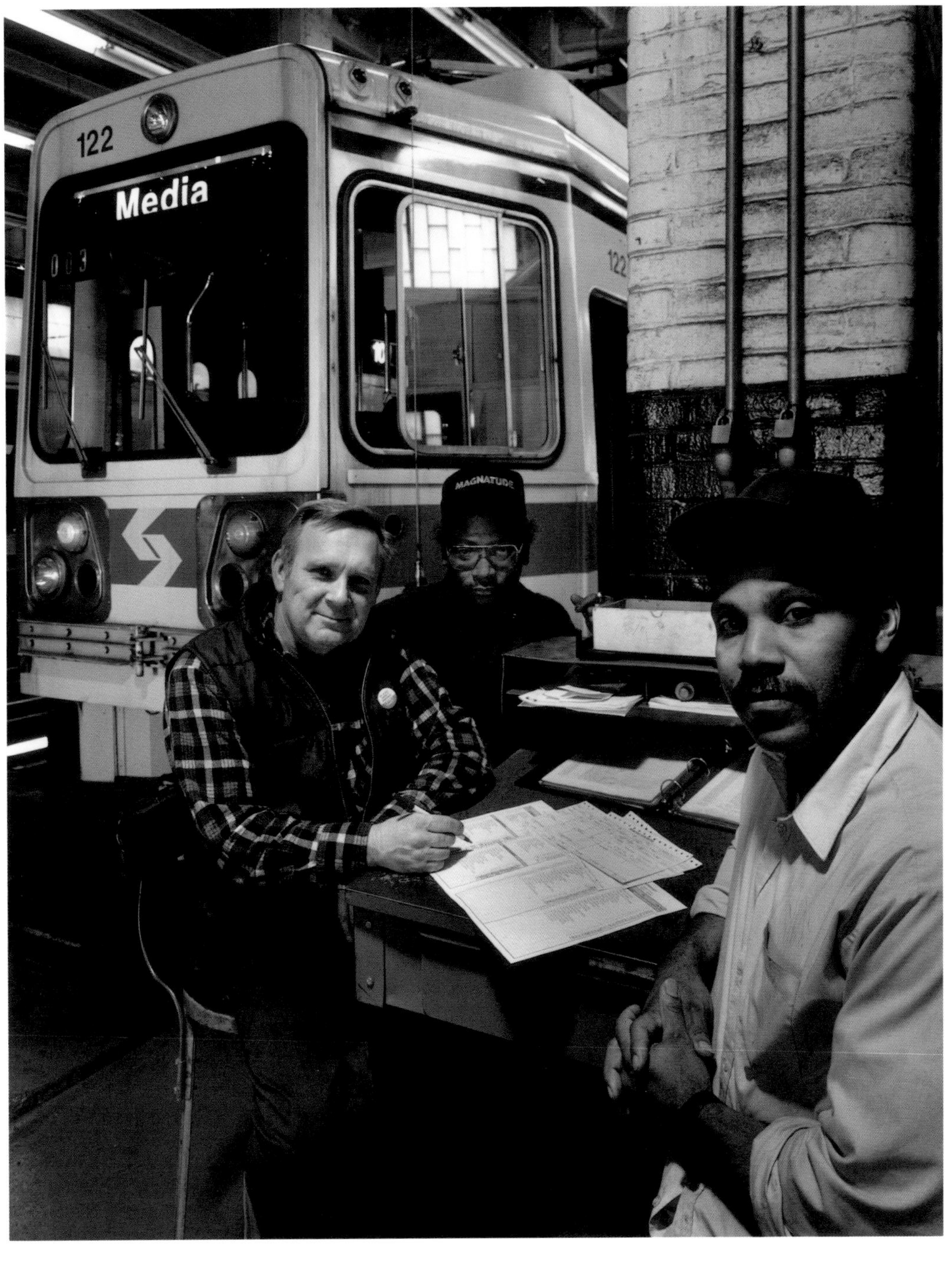

DON BARNA, ROY BELCHER, AND JAMES DAVID SMITH IN THE 69TH STREET SHOPS.

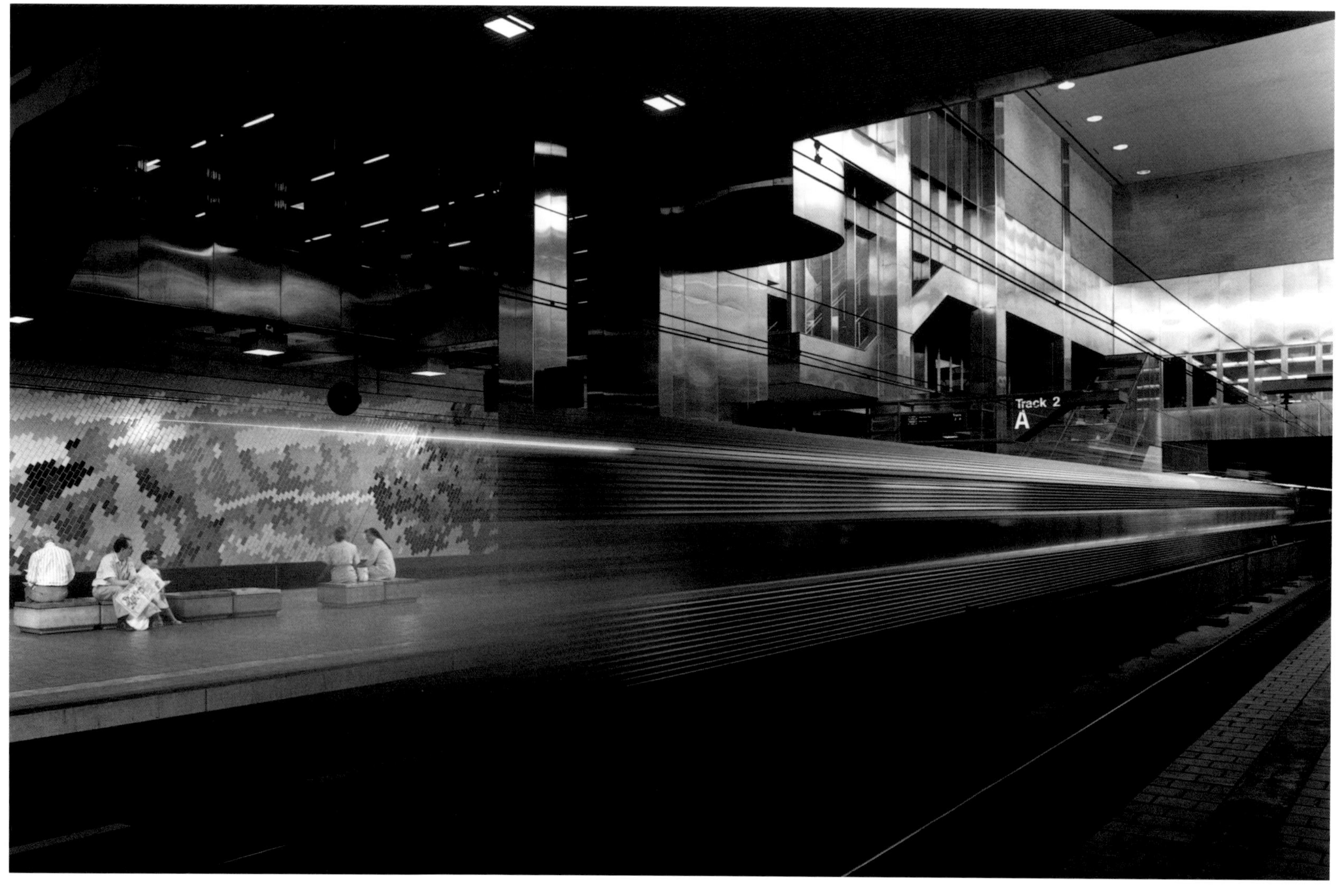

THE MARKET EAST STATION ON THE REGIONAL RAIL LINES OPENED IN 1984.

RIGHT: MAIN WAITING ROOM OF THE 69TH STREET TERMINAL.

Route 100
Rts 1,65,103,105,106

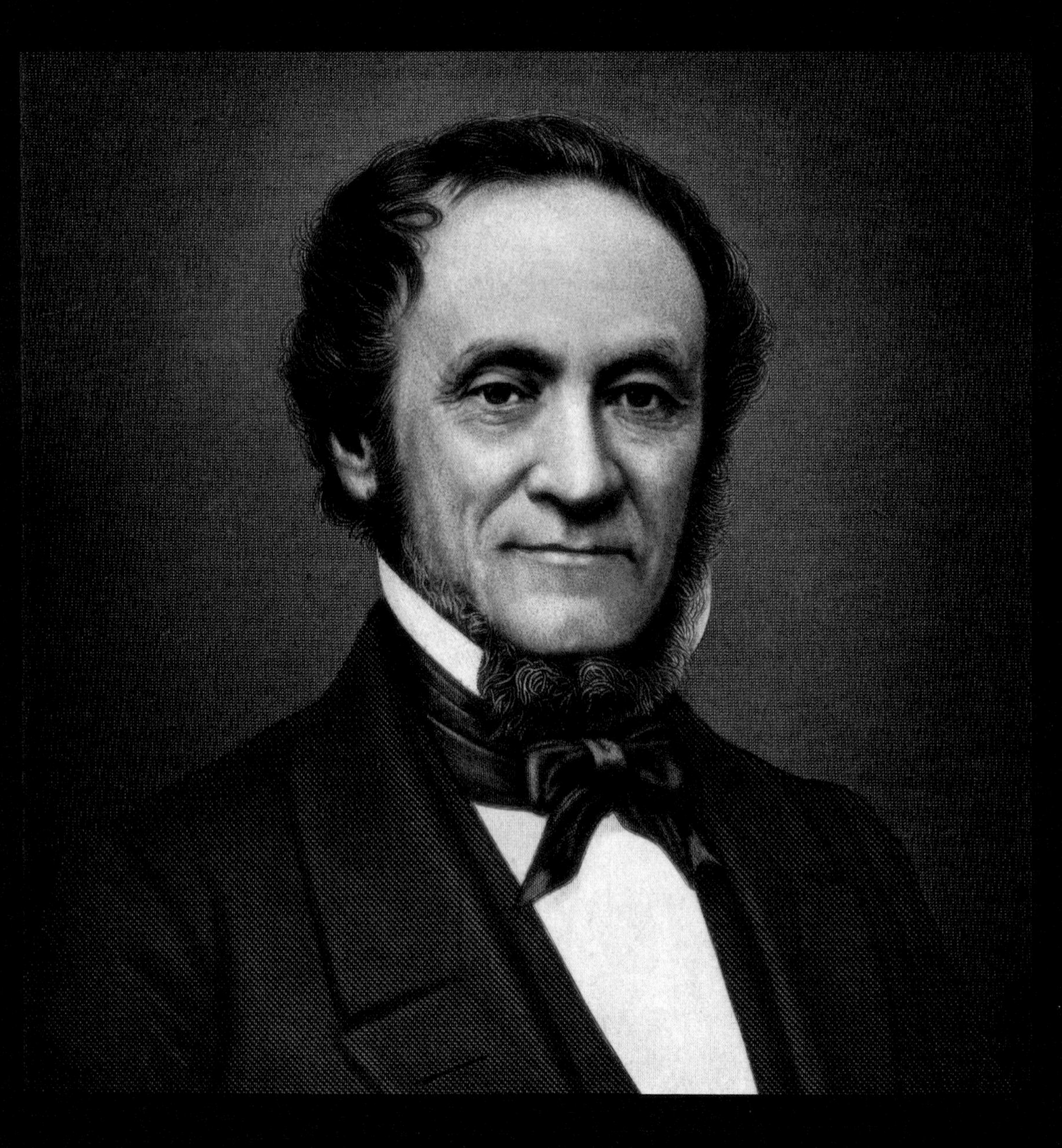

FROM WATER PIPES TO HOAGIES:

SURVIVAL THROUGH CREATIVE ADAPTATION AT WAWA

RICHARD DAVIS WOOD (1799–1869) MADE HIS FIRST FORTUNE AS A WHOLESALE DRYGOODS MERCHANT, THEN EXPANDED INTO COTTON AND IRON MANUFACTURING.

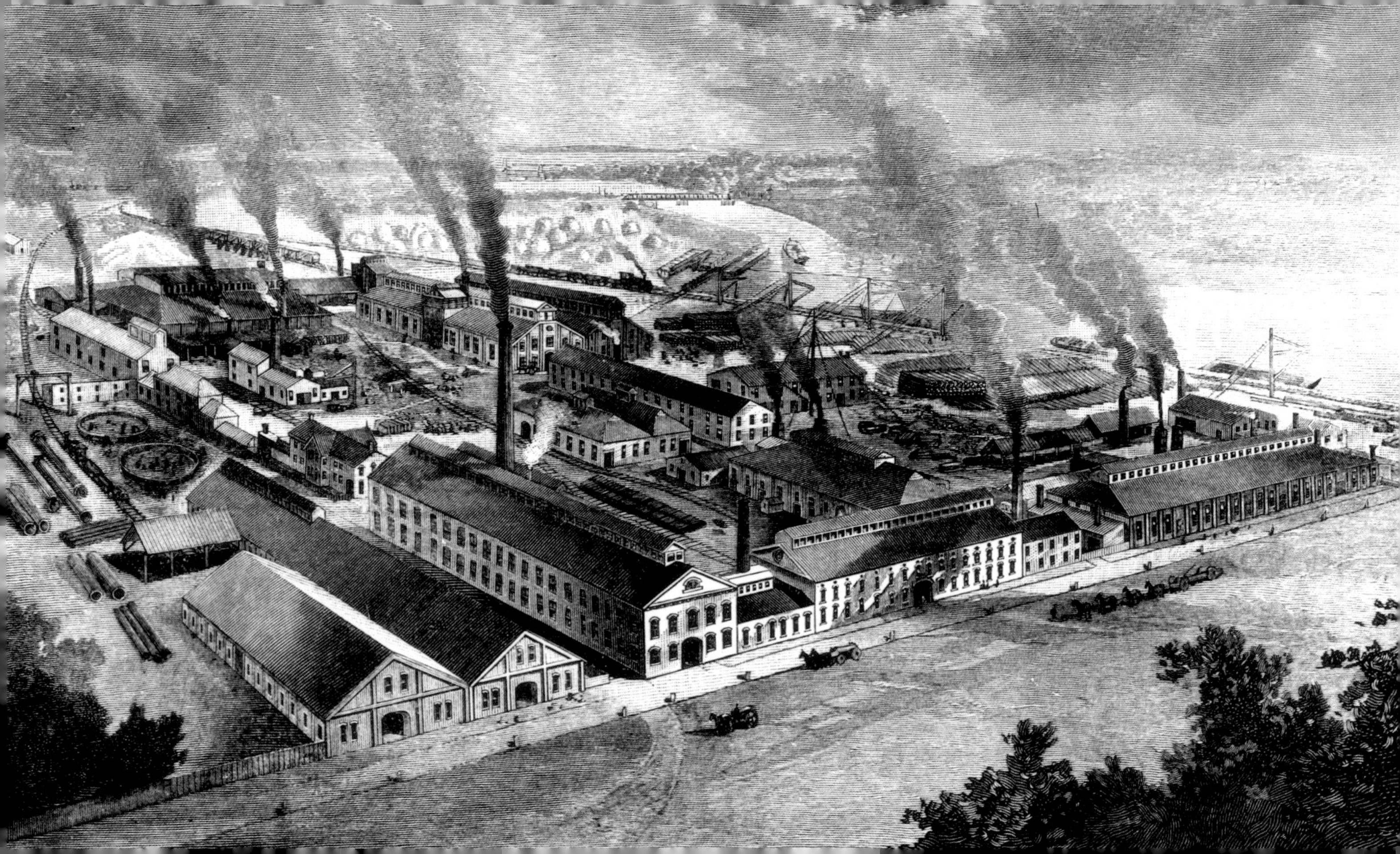

In the Philadelphia of 130 years ago, the name of Richard D. Wood would have stood for cotton textiles and iron, the twin pillars of the early industrial revolution. Today, Richard D. Wood's great-great-grandson and namesake is no longer a household name, even to the thousands of patrons of Wawa, the region's largest chain of convenience stores.

Richard D. Wood was born in 1799 in Cumberland County, New Jersey, a fifth-generation descendant of the great Quaker migration to the Delaware Valley more than a hundred years before. Richard D. Wood soon moved to Philadelphia and became a drygoods merchant. By the 1840s he was a respected leader of the city's business community, a founder of the Board of Trade, and a director of canals, railroads, banks, and insurance companies.

In 1849-1850, Richard's older half-brother, David C. Wood, found himself in financial difficulties. David had been in the iron business since 1803 and had constructed a blast furnace and foundry at Millville, New Jersey in 1814 for the manufacture of stove plates and cast iron pipe. The first cast iron pipe produced and sold in the United States was made in Millville. Richard knew little or nothing of the iron business, but the test of a good merchant was knowing when to buy, when to sell, and what would appreciate in value. He bought his half-brother's operation, including the vast tracts of woodland that had supplied the works with charcoal. Richard constructed a larger foundry and expanded the production of pipe and other iron castings. Capitalizing on his experience at Millville, Richard invested in other iron-manufacturing enterprises, including the Allentown Iron Company in the Lehigh Valley and the Cambria Iron Company at Johnstown. He leased the works in Johnstown under the partnership of Wood, Morrell & Company. During the eight years of the leasehold, they successfully transformed the company into the one of largest rolling mill complexes in the country.

Wood saw other potential at Millville. Long involved in the cotton trade, he decided to build his own cotton mill to use the excess waterpower. A mill containing 18,000 spindles and 350 looms was completed in 1854 and incorporated as The Millville Manufacturing Company eleven years later. A bleachery and window-glass factory followed in 1863-1864.

In 1859 Wood installed a new water turbine that was being promoted by Emile Geyelin. It performed so well, that Wood arranged to manufacture the turbines under license at his foundry, and Geyelin was associated with the Wood firm until his death in 1900.

In 1866-1868 Wood built a new, larger dam across the Maurice River, which greatly increased the horsepower available for his factories. Not content with this, he built a second cotton mill on the Egg Harbor River at Mays Landing in 1867. In the same year, Wood picked up another bargain when he purchased the Florence Iron Works from an unsuccessful operator. This plant was located on the east bank of the Delaware above Philadelphia and eventually became the center of the pipe-casting business.

When Richard D. Wood died in 1869, the family enterprises were inherited by his six sons. Over time, the third son, George Wood (1842-1926), assumed responsibility for the textile operations, while his younger brothers Walter and Stuart ran the iron foundries. In 1883 they purchased the Camden Iron Works. By 1890 the iron enterprises employed 1,300 men and turned out fire hydrants, lamp posts,

THE CAMDEN IRON WORKS, ESTABLISHED BY JOHN F. AND JESSE STARR IN 1849, WAS PURCHASED BY R. D. WOOD & COMPANY IN 1883. IT MANUFACTURED PIPES, PUMPS, TURBINES, AND GASOMETERS, SOME OF WHICH ARE VISIBLE IN THE OPEN AT THE FAR LEFT.

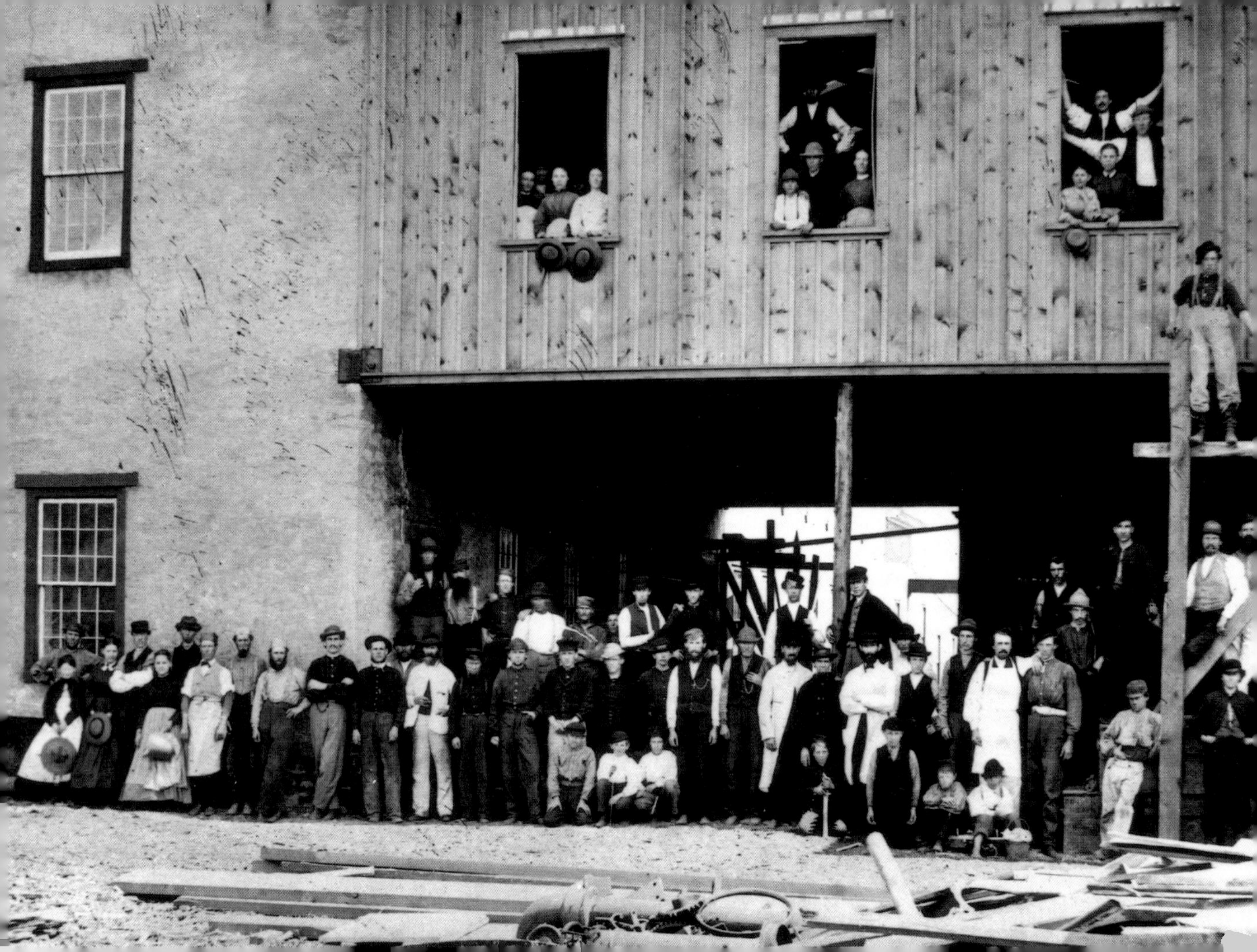

gasometers, pumps, and turbines, as well as pipe. The Millville foundry closed in the late 1890s, and the Camden Iron Works was shut down in 1924. The Florence foundry ceased to be a family business after the death of Walter Wood in 1934. However, it continued to operate under the R. D. Wood name until 1962, when it became part of the Griffin Pipe Products Division of Amstead Industries of Chicago. It still specializes in cast iron water and drain pipe, providing the piping for new suburbs like Levittown in the 1950s, just as its predecessors had done for Philadelphia in the early 1800s.

Under George Wood, The Millville Manufacturing Company prospered. At its peak in the 1910s and 1920s it employed more than 1,500 men, women, and children. Originally the firm produced cotton sheeting and stock for the garment trades, but by the 1930s and 1940s it was best known for "Red Star Nursery Products."

Around 1890 George Wood bought land for a summer retreat in a then-rural part of Delaware County west of Media and bought a small herd of Guernsey cows. Like his father, George was not one to miss an opportunity, and what might have been another man's hobby became a commercial business. Wawa Dairy Farms began production in 1902, offering certified raw milk. The name Wawa was a Native-American word for the Canada goose in flight, as quoted in Longfellow's popular "Song of Hiawatha." Wood's dairy opened before pasteurization had been adopted on a large scale, and Wawa milk was raw milk that was regularly inspected and "certified" as safe by doctors. In 1929 the company built a modern milk processing plant on Baltimore Pike in Wawa, Pennsylvania.

The Wood family enterprises spanned the entire spectrum of work environments, from the grit and molten metal of the casting floor and the pounding of forges and presses; through the textile factories, with their ranks of clattering spindles tended by women and children, the noisier and heavier looms worked by men, and the reeking vats of the bleachery; to the antiseptic, continuous flow production of the dairy and bottling plant; to the milkman on his solitary early morning rounds.

The economic and social changes that followed World War II had a profound impact on the Wood family firms. The textile business was declining under competition from lower-wage, non-union mills in the South. The dairy business had been allowed to stagnate since the Depression. George's grandsons revitalized the operation, aided by the postwar baby boom. In the decade after 1948 Wawa increased its number of home delivery routes from twenty to approximately 120, particularly in the suburbs, and absorbed the Brookmead, Crystle, Ardrossan, and Turner-Westcott Dairies.

By the early 1960s, conditions were once again critical. Attempts to keep the textile business competitive by buying some small southern mills had failed, and disposable diapers were replacing cloth ones. Supermarkets were replacing the neighborhood milkman. George's grandson, Grahame Wood (1915-1982), was determined to meet the competition by selling Wawa milk in his own chain of mini-markets. Convenience stores had been around since the 1920s, when the Southland Ice Company of Oak Cliff, Texas, the ancestor of today's 7-Eleven food stores, began selling bread and milk to augment its regular products. However, they were largely con-

EMPLOYEES AT THE BLEACHERY BREAK TO POSE FOR THE CAMERA AT THE MILLVILLE MANUFACTURING COMPANY, CA. 1880.

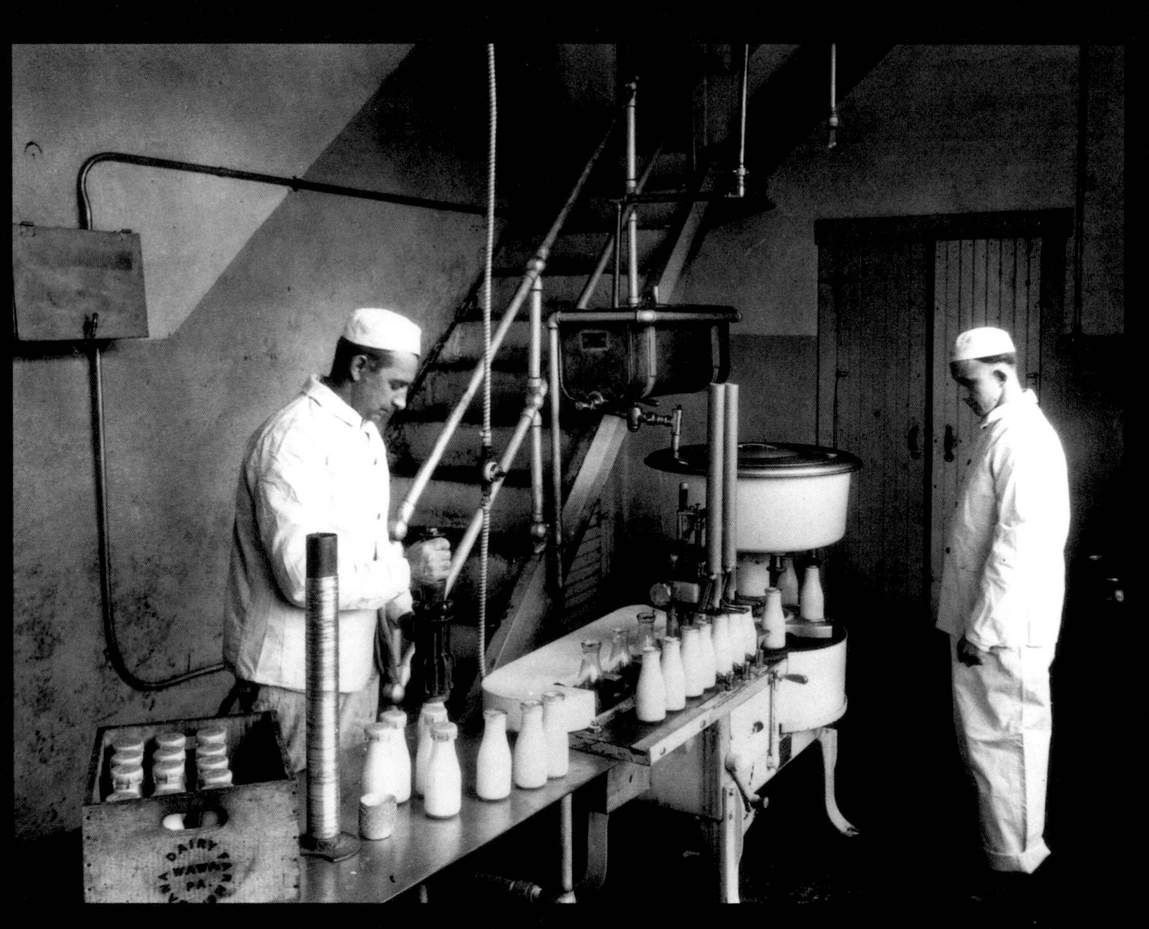
DAIRY
WAWA
PA

fined to the South and West, while towns and cities in the Northeast were served by numerous mom-and-pop stores and corner delicatessens. The newly-developing suburbs proved an ideal niche. The Millville textile business was liquidated between 1963 and 1965, and the first Wawa Food Market opened in Folsom, Pennsylvania in April 1964. The first store was a success and it heralded the beginning of Wawa's chain of food markets, now spanning five eastern states. The food markets and dairies operated under the charter of The Millville Manufacturing Company.

In 1968, the food market subsidiary had absorbed both the old Millville Manufacturing Company and the Wawa Dairy Farms. The corporate name was changed to Wawa, Inc. in 1974. The residual assets of the textile firm were used to finance expansion, and the old ironmaster's mansion built by David C. Wood became a Wawa regional office. By 1972 Wawa had 100 stores and was beginning to sell takeout coffee and sandwiches.

By aggressive marketing and careful attention to product lines and customer service, Wawa has become the largest convenience store chain in the Delaware Valley, with 500 stores in five states and more than 8,000 employees. Wawa Food Markets are highly specialized convenience stores that emphasize the sale of perishable products. Currently, Wawa distinguishes itself from other convenience stores by offering a large selection of delicatessen meats and cheeses, a broad offering in fresh produce, freshly made sandwiches, and a wide selection of its own ice cream and dairy products. Today, the old processing plant in Wawa, Pennsylvania has been expanded to include the brick dairy plant and a large warehouse complex which supplies more than 50 percent of the products sold in the Wawa Food Markets. A fleet of Wawa trucks serves the stores daily.

BOTTLE-FILLING AT THE OLD DAIRY PLANT AT WAWA, CA. 1925, SHOWN HERE FOUR YEARS BEFORE THE PRESENT PLANT OPENED. GLASS MILK BOTTLES WERE SEALED WITH WAX PAPER AND WIRE CAPS.

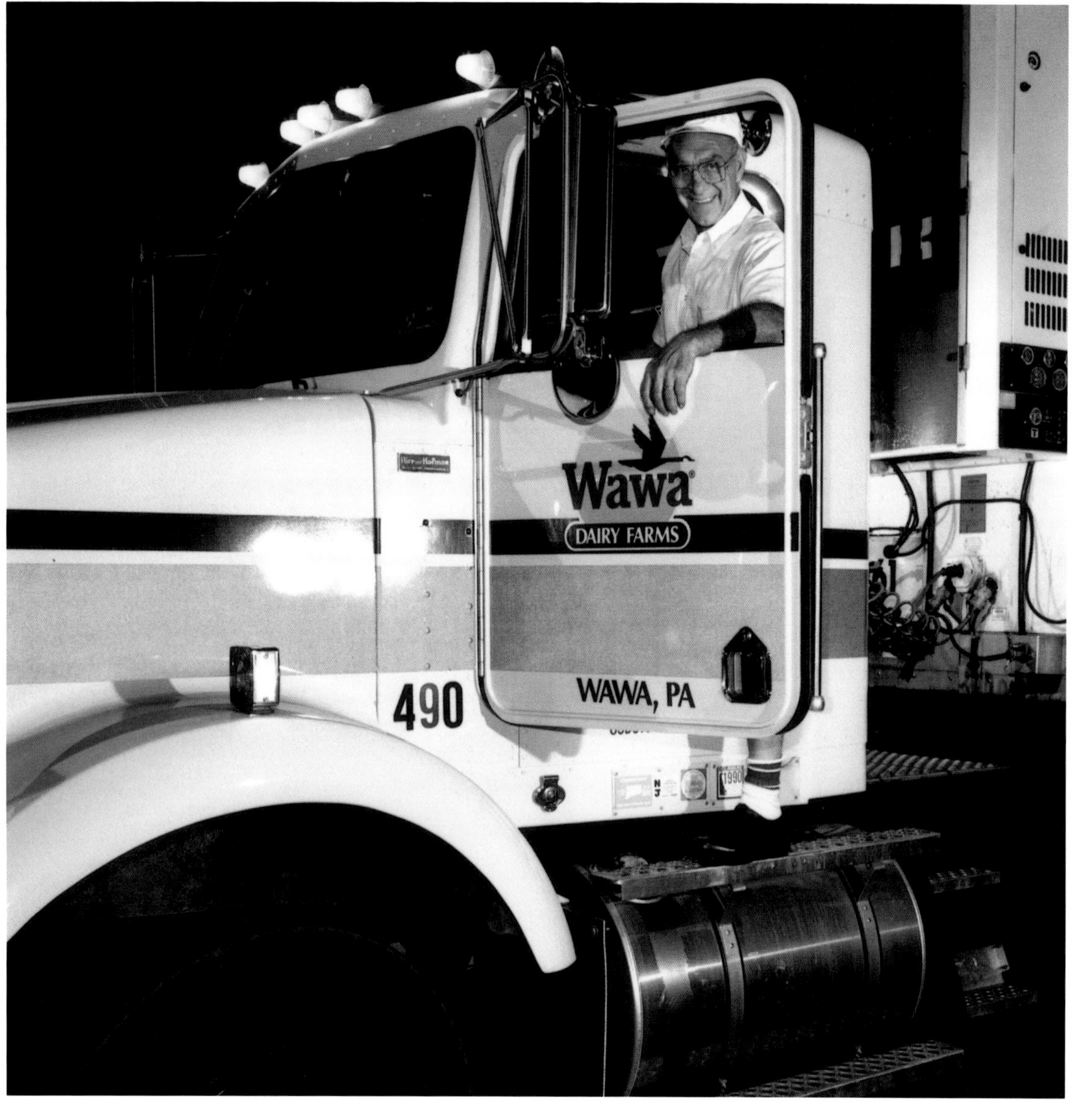

ARMANDO MADDESI AT THE DAIRY WAREHOUSE DISTRIBUTION COMPLEX NEAR MIDNIGHT.

RIGHT: BESSY GURST AND MARY WONTROBA IN CENTRAL COMPUTING ROOM OF WAWA'S HEADQUARTERS.

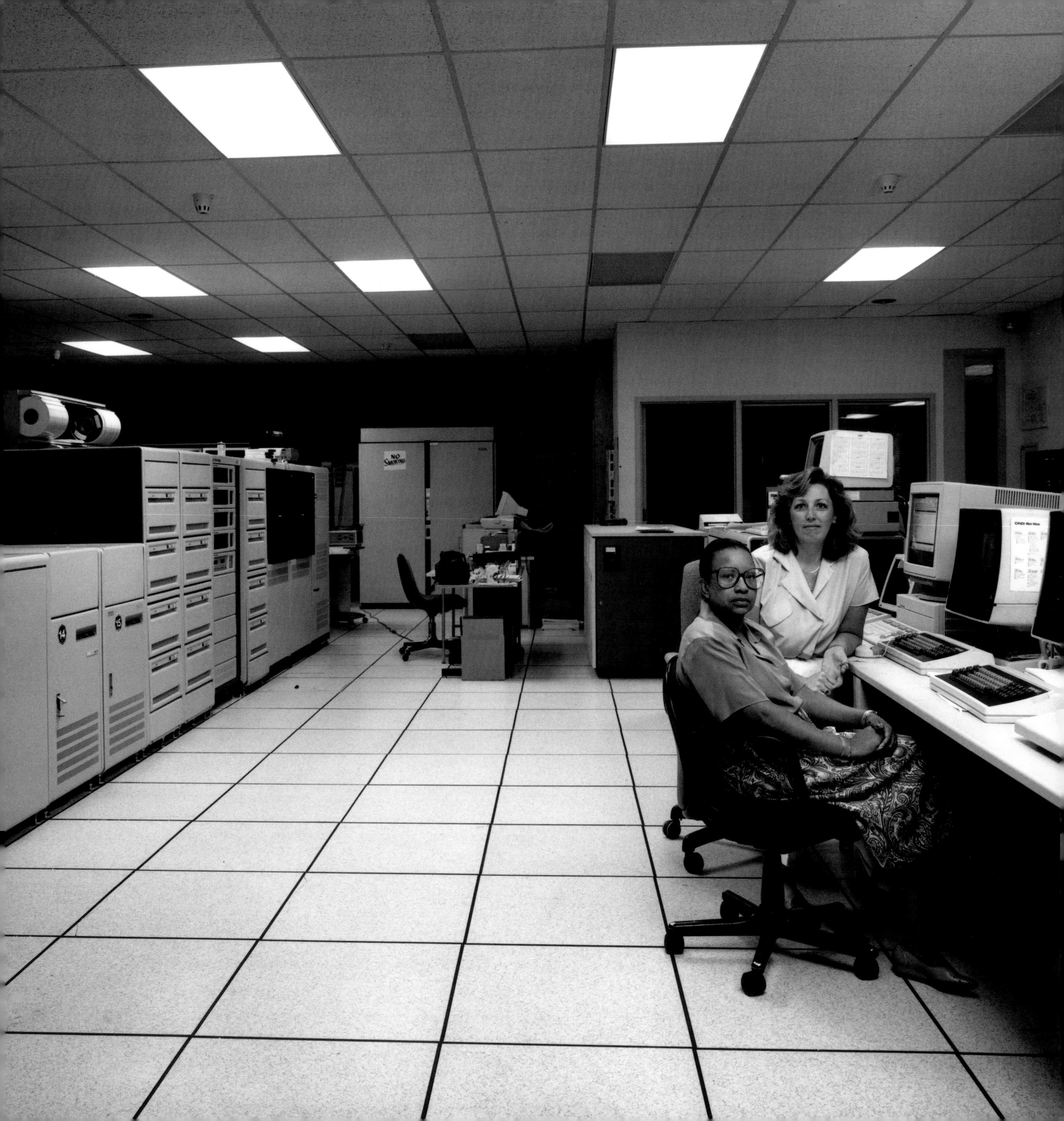
NO SMOKING
14
15

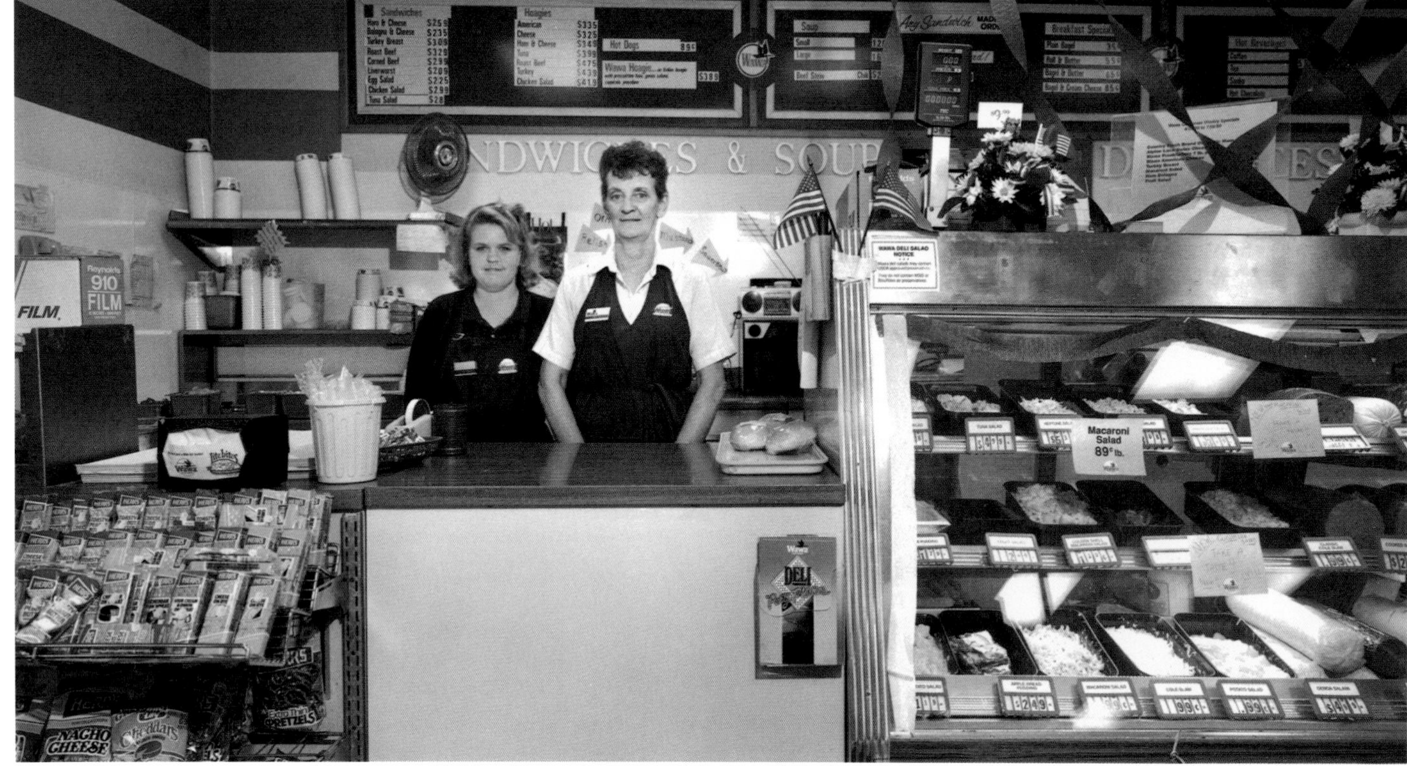

GRETCHEN ANDREWS
AND ANITA O'DONNELL AT
A WAWA MARKET IN
MILLVILLE, NEW JERSEY.

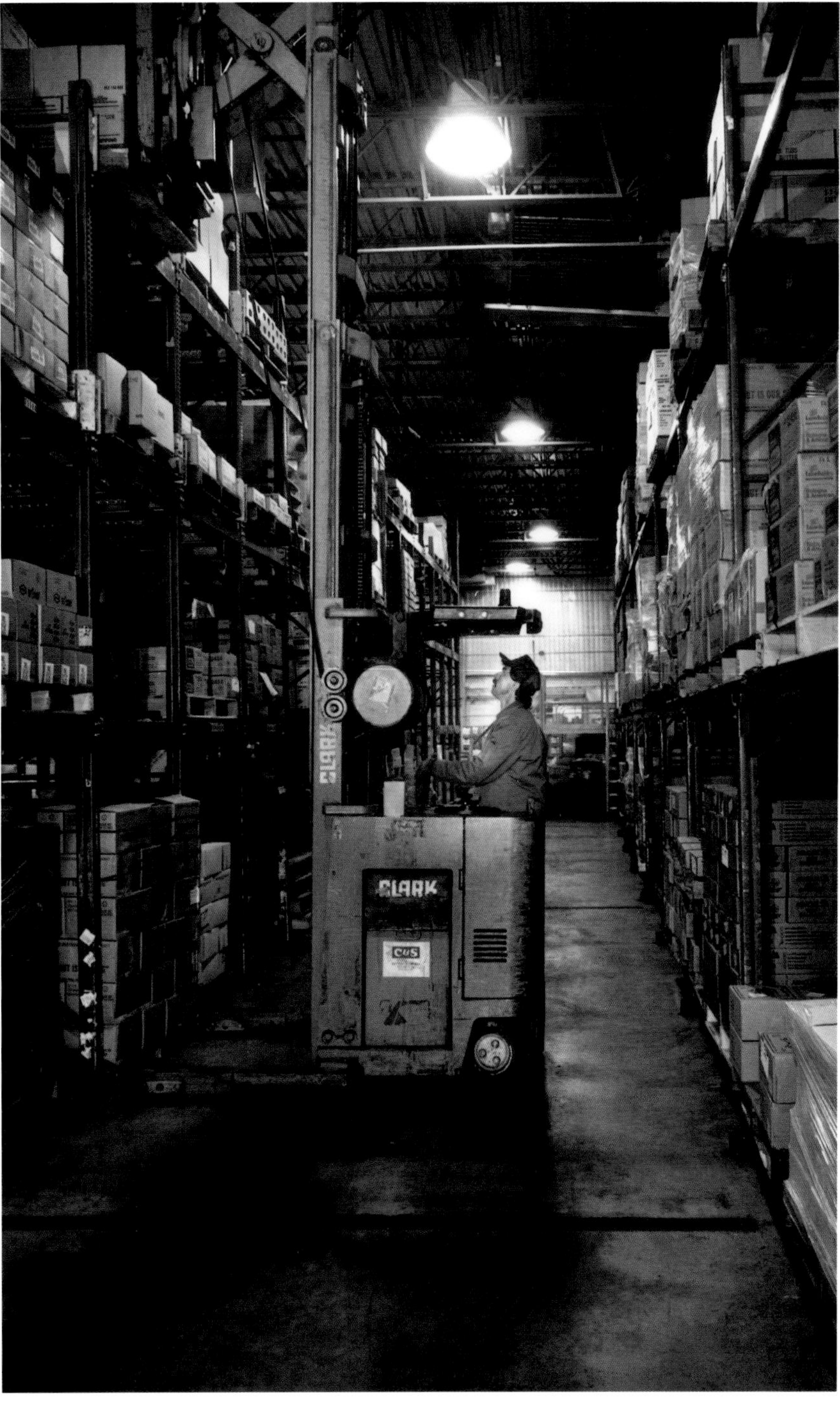

MOVING DELICATESSEN MEATS IN WAWA'S PERISHABLES WAREHOUSE.

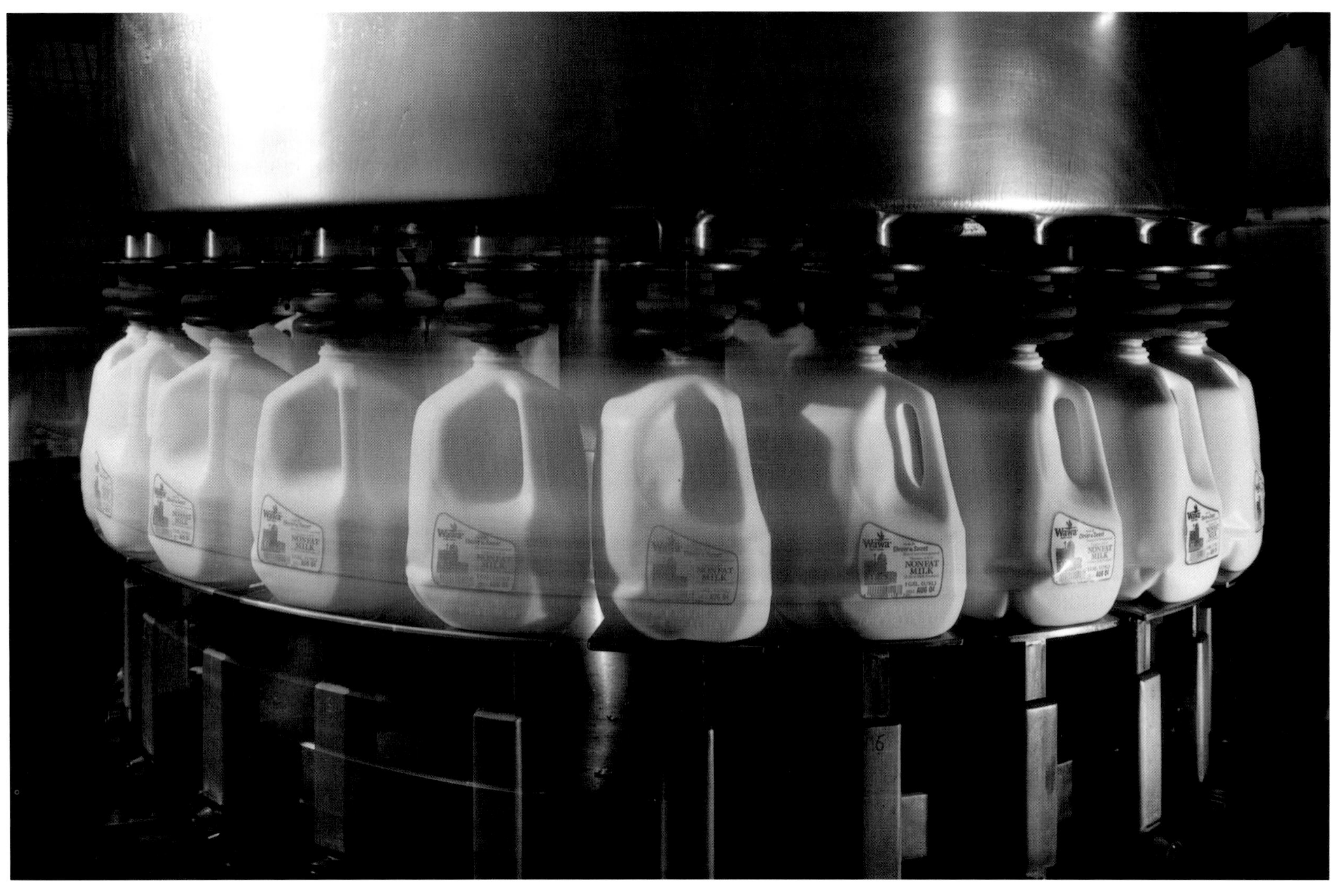

PLASTIC GALLON CONTAINERS BEING FILLED WITH MILK AT THE WAWA DAIRY.

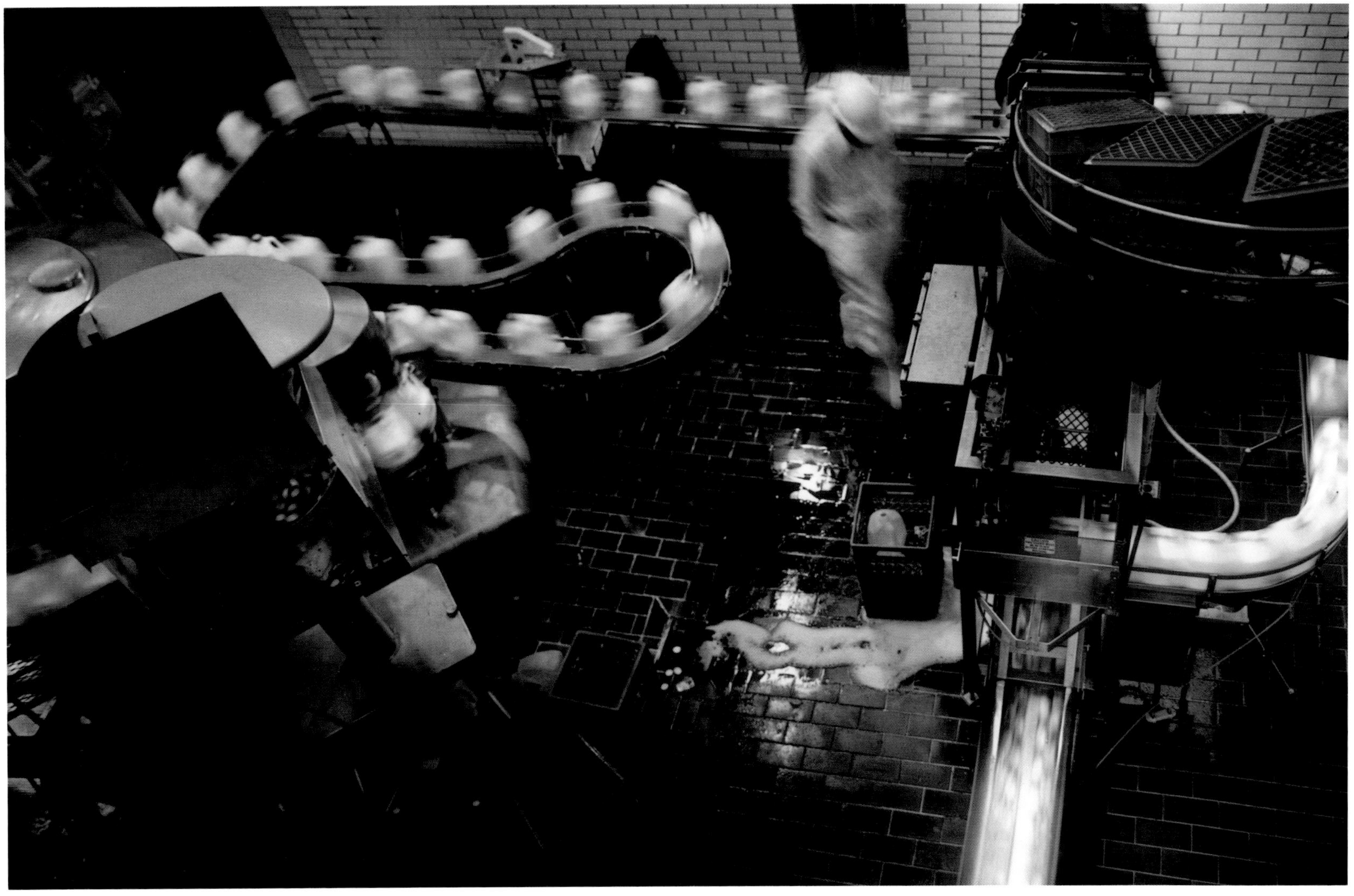

OVERHEAD VIEW
OF THE ONE-GALLON
FILLING LINE AT
WAWA DAIRY PLANT.

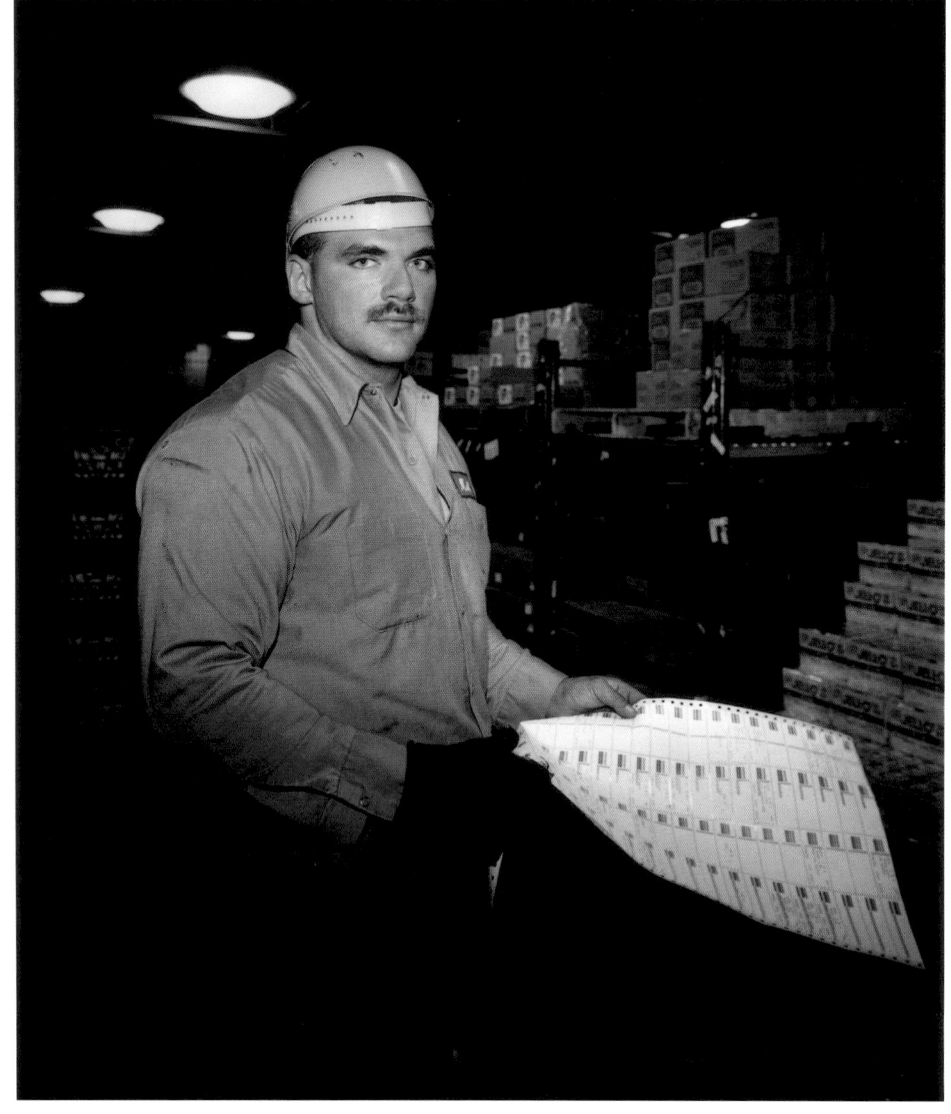

MATT DEPORTER, A WAREHOUSE WORKER AT THE COMPANY'S PERISHABLES WAREHOUSE.

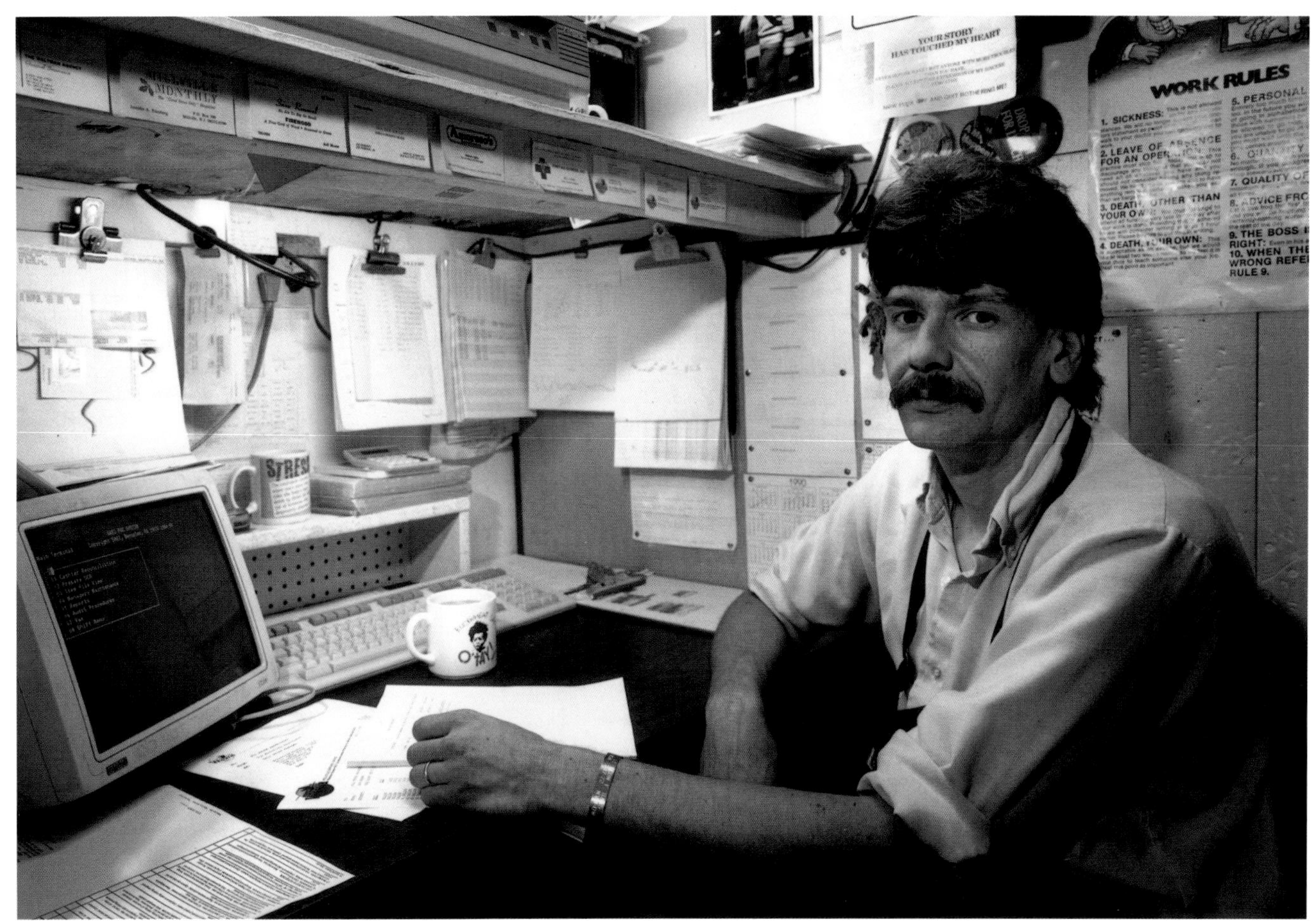

MIKE KANE, MANAGER OF THE WAWA MARKET IN MILLVILLE, NEW JERSEY.

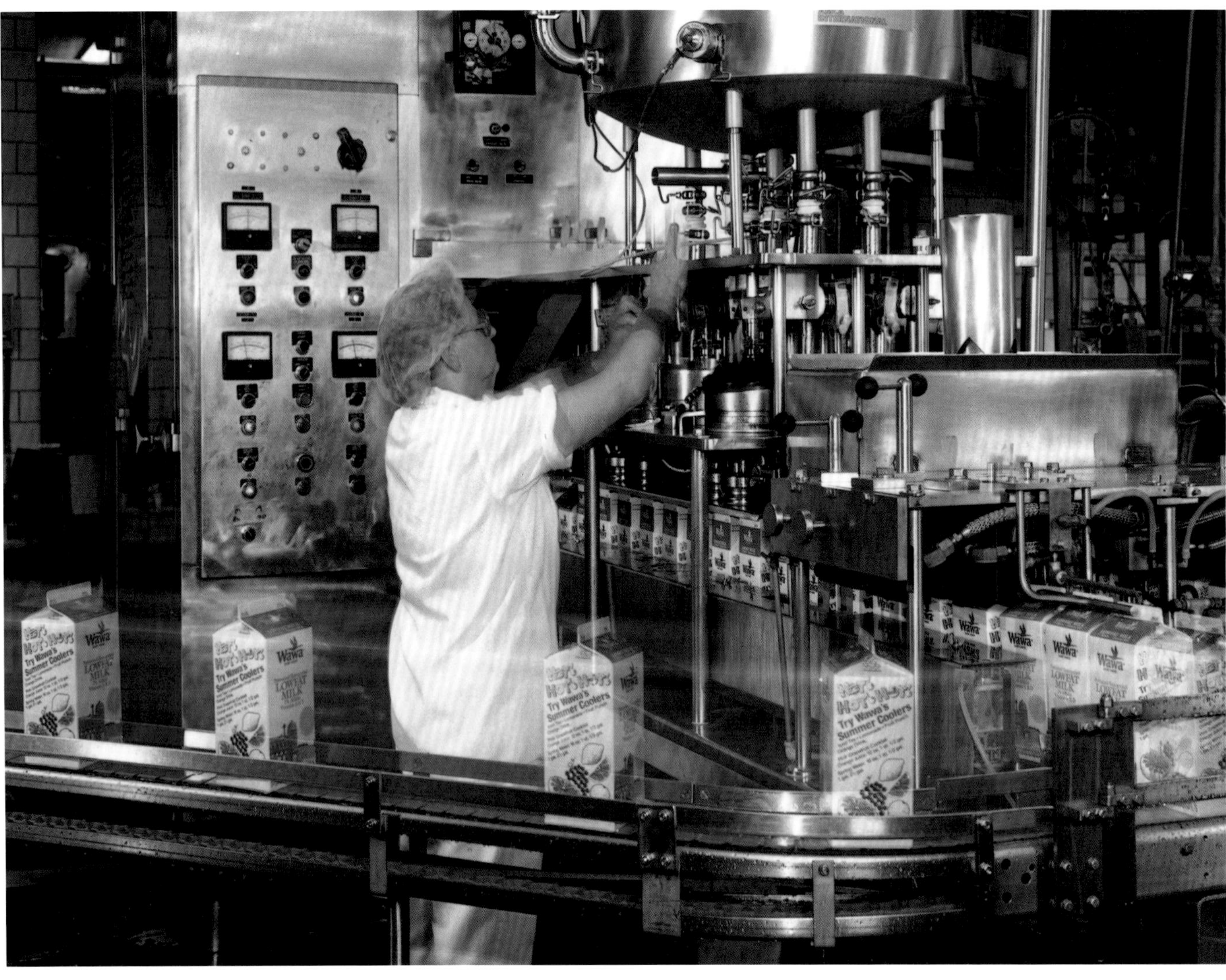

ETHEL TYERS, A THIRTY-SEVEN-YEAR VETERAN, MONITORS SEALING AND DATE STAMPING.

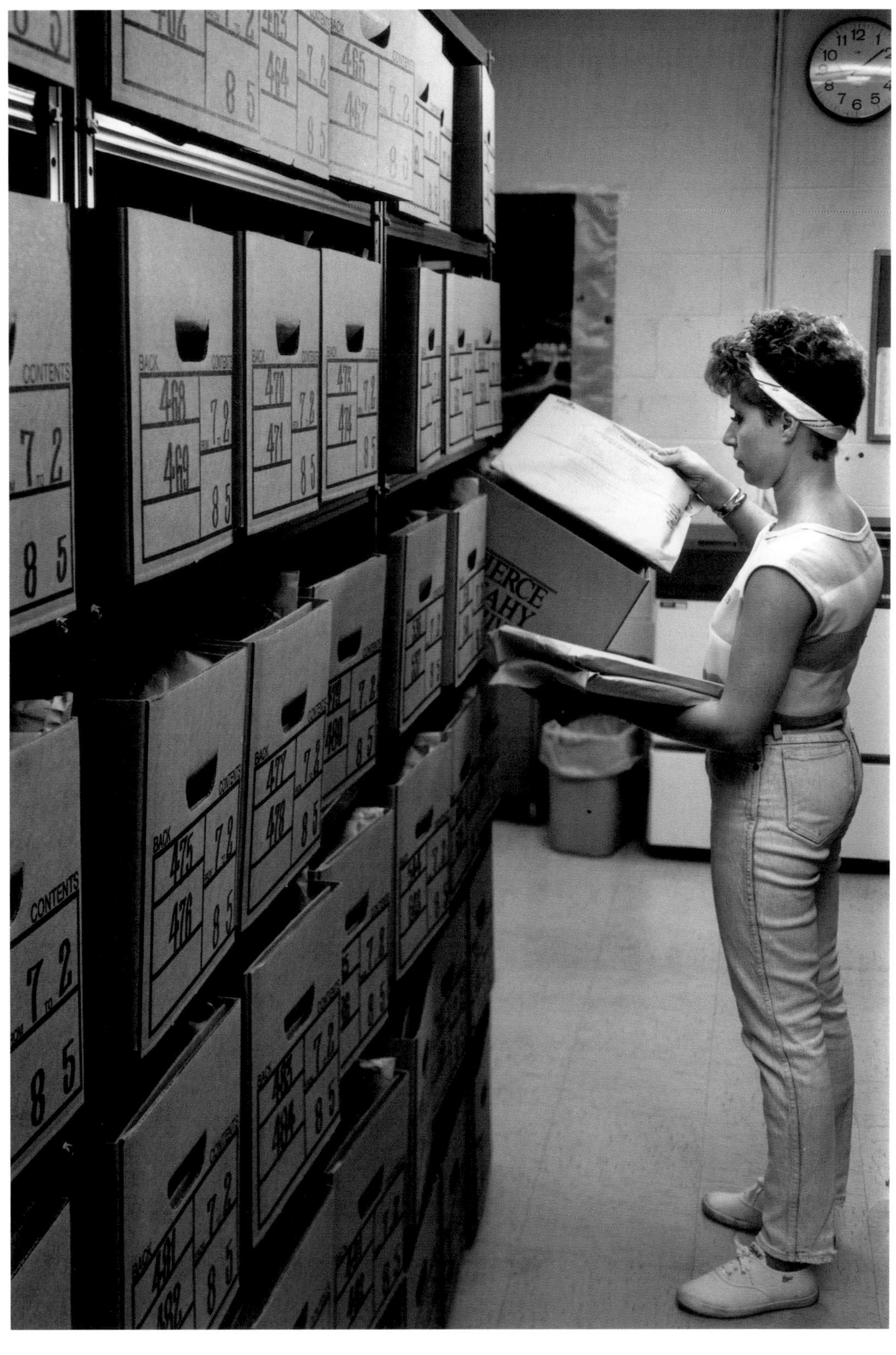

JOANNE COLLISON SORTS MAIL AT WAWA'S "RED ROOF" CORPORATE HEADQUARTERS.

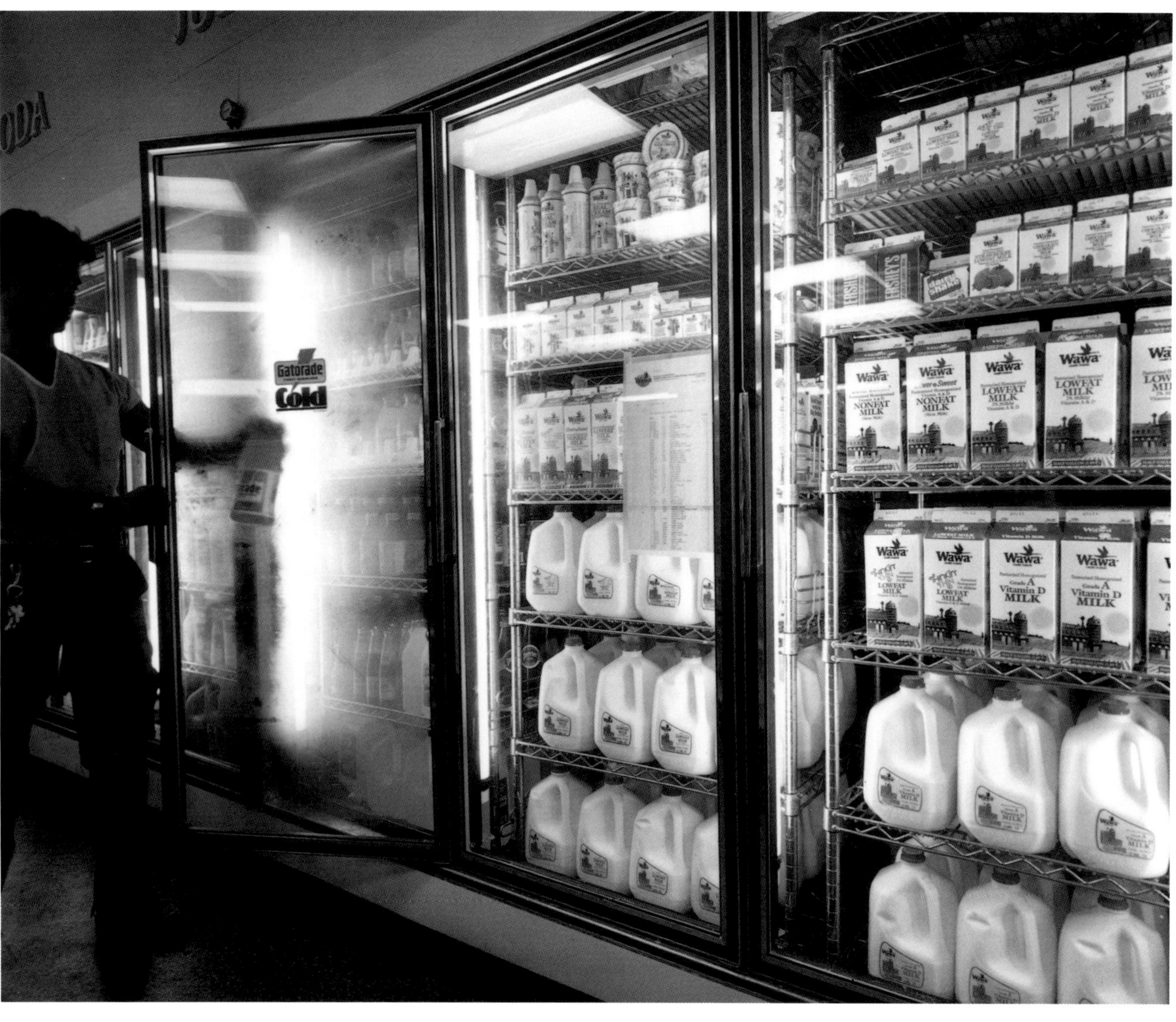

DAIRY CASES DISPLAY
A VARIETY OF PRODUCTS
AT A WAWA MARKET IN
MILLVILLE, NEW JERSEY.

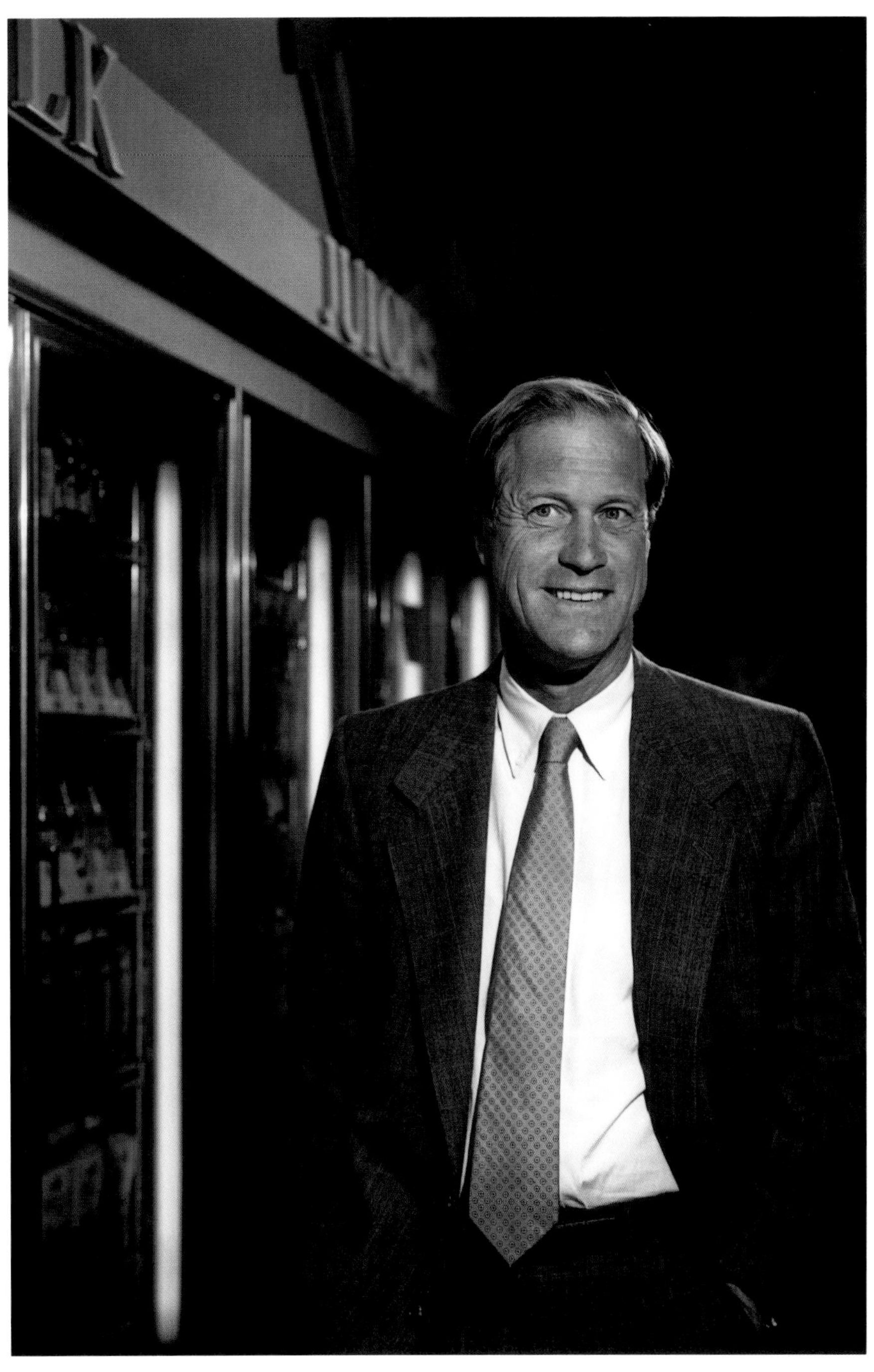

RICHARD D. WOOD, JR., PRESIDENT AND CHIEF EXECUTIVE OFFICER OF WAWA, INC. SINCE 1977.

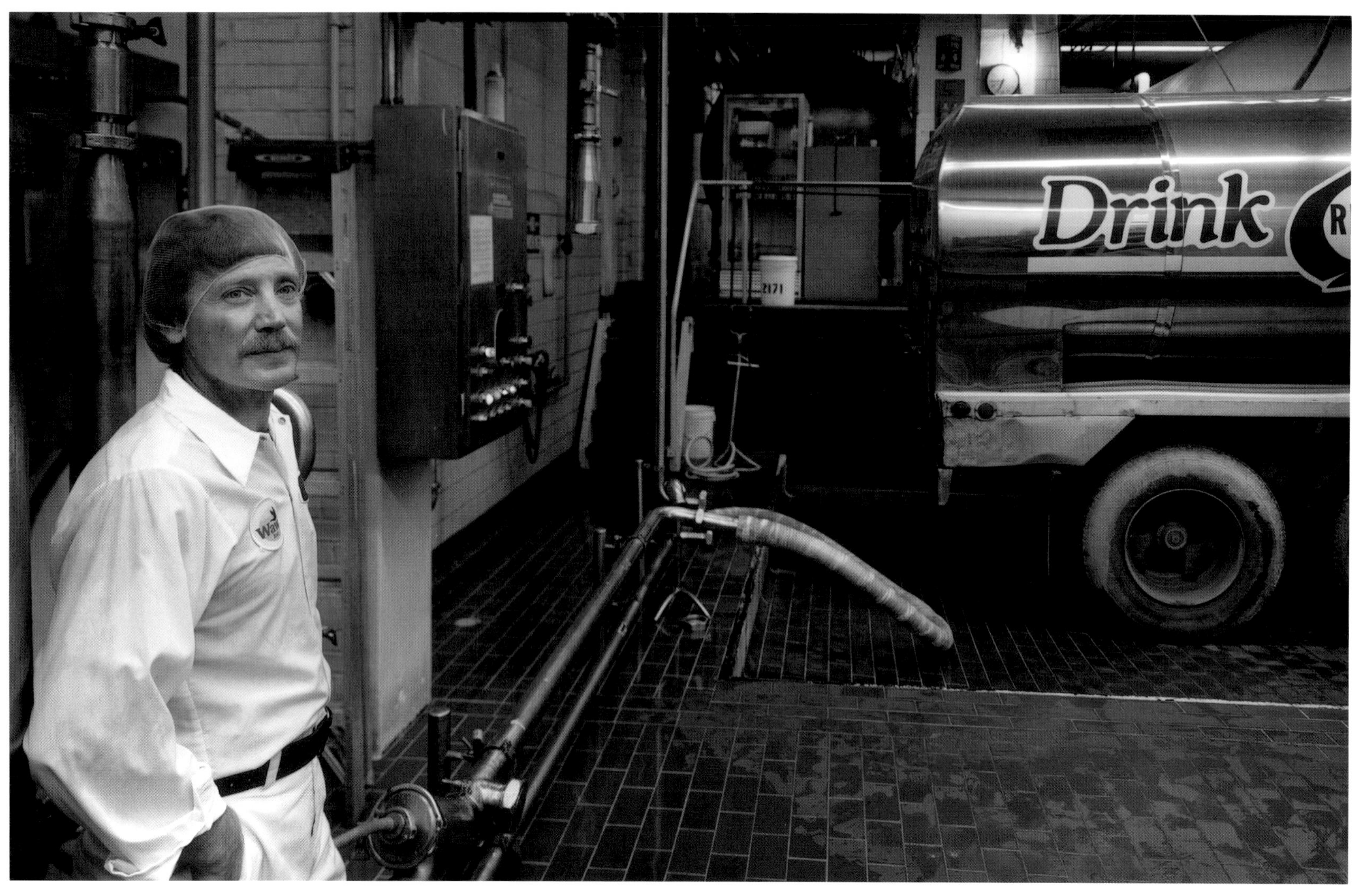

JIM ROSE, MILK RECEIVER, AT WAWA'S DAIRY PLANT.

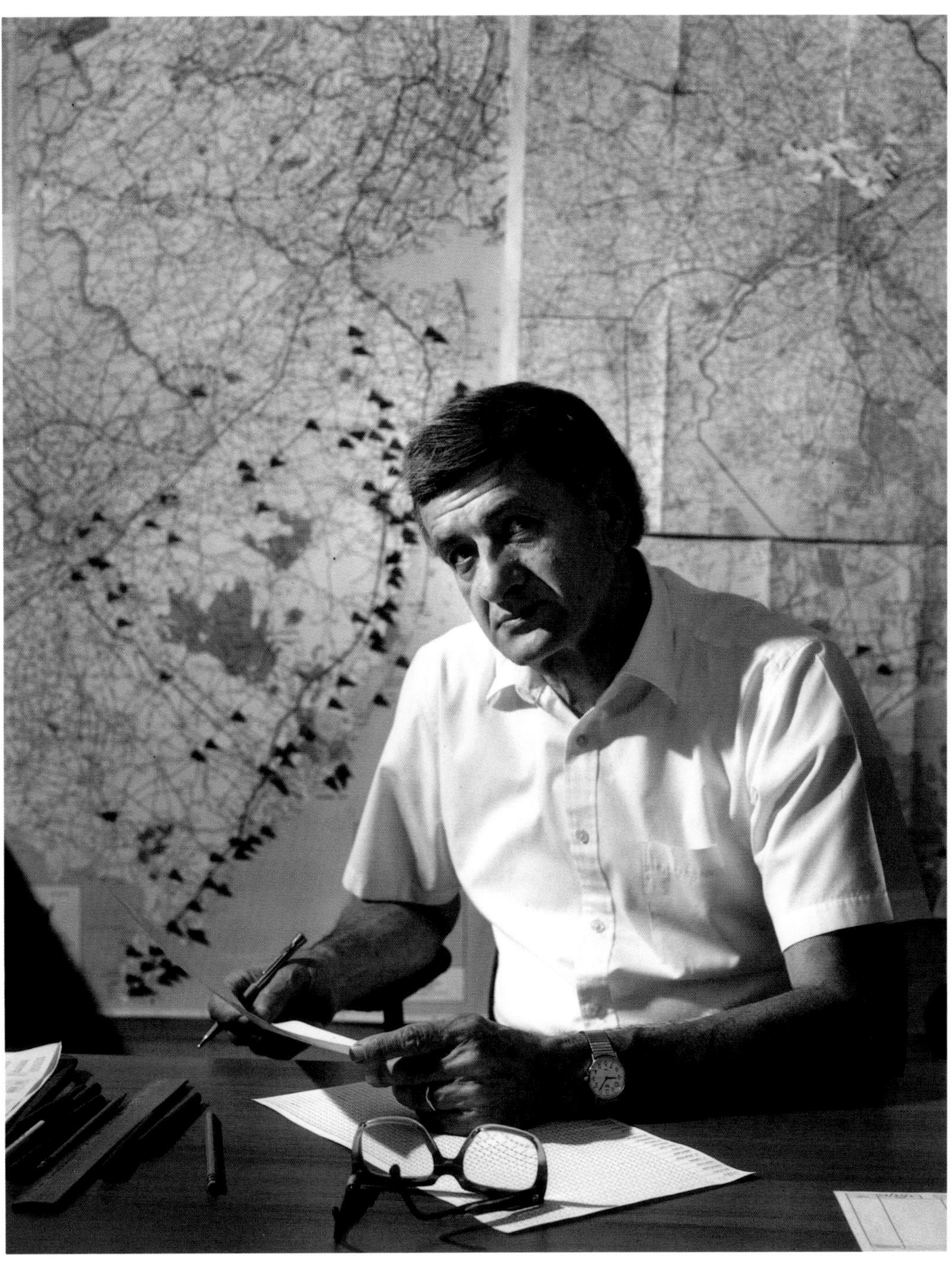

PAT PIPINO,
HEAD DISPATCHER IN
WAWA'S TRANSPOR-
TATION DEPARTMENT.

Baldwin, Boeing, Lukens, SEPTA, and Wawa are many things: congregations of people, buildings, logos, landscapes, the morning coffee, the ride to work. They are also all case studies in entrepreneurship, in that each was formed and shaped by an individual or a succession of individuals.

Innovations, technologies, and businesses do not emerge spontaneously from the times—they require human midwives. Baldwin did not invent the locomotive, but he determined what successful locomotives would look like and where they would be built. The same was true of Piasecki and the helicopter. Philadelphia was not predetermined to be an engine-building center. Paterson, New Jersey, Lima, Ohio, and Schenectady, New York, all produced locomotives that were at one time the equals or betters of Baldwin's, and all of Philadelphia's many competing builders quickly failed. Grahame Wood and his successors did not invent the convenience store, but they did give it a distinctive character, and as a result, the profits are not exported to other regions.

These firms were built by different kinds of entrepreneurs. Baldwin, Piasecki, and Isaac Pennock came from a craft or technical tradition and were able to translate their skills into profits and so continue their experimentations. The Woods were fundamentally merchants who enjoyed buying and selling, particularly down-to-earth essentials like iron pipe, steel rails, motors, cotton cloth, milk or daily bread. Taylor was a patrician lawyer with middle-class reform impulses, a grandnephew of the founder of Bryn Mawr College, interested in developing the suburban area where the family had long lived. Widener and Elkins were classic empire builders.

For success, however, one skill was usually not enough. Baldwin successfully worked with financial and managerial associates, while Widener and Mitten ran afoul of their bankers. The family firms of the Woods, Taylors, Lukenses, and Hustons relied on internal financing through retained earnings and a credit rating backed by sound performance. The Woods and Taylors hired technicians and managers or trained their children to fill the posts.

As befits the Delaware Valley context, three of our entrepreneurial families, the Woods, Taylors, and Lukenses, are of old Quaker stock, although the Hustons who followed Rebecca Lukens were, like Baldwin, devout Presbyterians. It is probably no accident that theirs were all successful family firms with a decidedly "Friendly" character: intimate scale, unpretentious, diligent, relatively informal, paternalistic, and consensus-oriented.

Other measurements of success are more ambiguous. Matthias Baldwin's statue stands with those of other worthies in front of City Hall, but the former Baldwin site is tellingly occupied by the *Philadelphia Inquirer* and *Daily News,* the Commonwealth office building, and the Community College. P.A.B. Widener amassed a fortune in excess of $30 million, not all of it from PRT, but his son and grandson were lost on the *Titanic* three years before his death. Perhaps a quarter of the Widener fortune was returned to his hometown in the form of various benefactions, but his superb art collection went to the National Gallery out of spite.

Mitten's personal fortune was less than a tenth of Widener's. His efforts to share the largesse with his employees were genuine. Harvard's Widener Library was a family gift. Temple's Mitten Hall was built by the voluntary contributions of his employees. Still, all of Mitten's good intentions and entrepreneurial savvy were ultimately unavailing in a period of stagnation.

There are, of course, social consequences to success. A successful entrepreneur brings together people, money, and talent to create goods and perform services. Successful businesses create jobs, subcultures, and communities. The creation of Wawa Food Markets created more jobs than existed in the old dairy and cotton mills, including store managers, buyers, truckers, and inventory control workers. Despite the loss of jobs to automation and foreign competition, steel is still being made in Coatesville. Red Arrow helped to create the Delaware County suburbs.

Whatever the measure, success for the entrepreneur is often a matter of chance, not just the random luck of the draw, but the ability to recognize opportunity when it knocks. For Baldwin and Piasecki, the possibilities were perhaps self-evident, although Baldwin had to wait three years between his first and second locomotive orders. On the other hand, Dr. Charles Huston had been raised in a family of physicians with a professional culture indifferent if not hostile to commerce. Only when ill health exiled him to rural Coatesville did he take an interest in the rolling mill that he eventually transformed into a modern enterprise. Richard D. Wood seems to have been particularly adept at recognizing the potential of whatever came his way. Grahame Wood's decision to build convenience stores was not a blind leap, but was supported by advice from the Breyers Ice Cream Company which had shelved its own plan for a similar chain of ice cream parlors, and from other friends with experience in the business. In contrast, Widener and Mitten were both betrayed by their daring and sense of optimism, if to strikingly different degrees. Still, each had to make the decisions and persuade others to follow.

Finally, these studies demonstrate that successful firms must be reinvented every second or third generation. Of our examples, the Wood family has been the most adept at this. Lukens Steel has been reinvented many times, first by Dr. Huston and his sons, then by the generation of the 1930s who adopted arc-welding and clad steels, then by the professional managers of the 1950s who cultivated markets opened by the Cold War and the space race. Baldwin's demise stems from the failure of Samuel Vauclain, a grand old man rooted in the nineteenth century and the builder of the white elephant that was Eddystone, to successfully reinvent the firm. He saw the promise of the diesel, but could probably not imagine a world in which GE and GM would build the relatively few diesels that were needed. His successors were forced to reinvent Baldwin-Lima-Hamilton without the locomotives. SEPTA still engaged in reinventing the transit system, a necessary public service that people have always demanded but have always been reluctant to pay for. Even as these photographs were being taken, each of the enterprises was changing, planning, reacting. For the survivors, reinvention is ongoing.

A C K N O W L E D G M E N T

We are grateful to The Lukens Foundation and to Wawa, Inc. for providing major funding for this project.

I would like to thank the many people at Boeing, Lukens, SEPTA, and Wawa, Inc. who made this book possible. Their good humor in allowing me to photograph them was the most important element in this project. Without their cooperation these photographs would have been impossible to make.

Key individuals assisted me at each organization. Sam Farrell's intimate knowledge was indispensable at Boeing, and Walt Myers's help made the old Baldwin site accessible. Charles Brown and Raymond Paget opened all doors at Lukens Steel. John F. Tucker III used his intimate knowledge of SEPTA to help me produce a clear picture of the conditions at this public transportation giant. Maria Thompson's work on the history of the Wawa company, her concern for the preservation of historic materials and her entree to Wawa, Inc. made this section possible.

The search for historic images was aided by: Janice Dockery and Louise Jones at the Historical Society of Pennsylvania; Ben Kline at the Railroad Museum of Pennsylvania; Robert Eskin at the Atwater Kent Museum; and Ron DeGraw who donated the Red Arrow collection and helped me find the right people at SEPTA. Hagley Fellow Regina Blaszczyk's assistance with research and verifying information on the photographs was instrumental in the completion of this undertaking.

I would like to thank everyone at the Hagley Museum and Library. I would like to thank especially fellow photographer Charles Foote. Charles's back-up work and beautiful historical prints were critical to this project. I am grateful to Jill MacKenzie for keeping the book on track. Finally I would like to thank Jon Williams and Glenn Porter for their support and understanding. — Martin W. Kane

The Hagley Museum and Library, located in Wilmington, Delaware, is a nonprofit educational institution dedicated to the preservation and understanding of America's economic and technological heritage. Located on the site of the original Du Pont Company black powder works, Hagley is one of the nation's leading industrial museums and is accredited by the American Association of Museums. The library is recognized internationally as a repository for business and technological history and is a member of the Independent Research Libraries Association.

Martin W. Kane has been involved in photography for the past twenty years, having begun his career with the Chilton Book Company as an editor and photographer. He worked for a Knight-Ridder Newspaper, the *Macon Telegraph and News,* before devoting himself full-time to independent photography in 1981. He has been a staff photographer with Hagley Museum and Library since 1983. During his time at Hagley, Kane has been documenting men and women in their work environment and adding to the body of industrial photography. It is out of these projects that the book and exhibit, *Works: Photographs of Enterprise*, has evolved. In addition to his work at Hagley, Kane has continued his independent work and produced exhibits such as *A Matter of Vision: Community Development in the Philadelphia Area and Excerpts 1979 to 1989.*

Christopher T. Baer has been associated with the Hagley Museum and Library since 1977, beginning with the production of *Mid-Atlantic Canals and Railroads,* a historical atlas published in 1981 and the 1979 exhibit "Little Machines". He has subsequently worked for Hagley's manuscripts and archives department where he has organized a number of Hagley's largest industrial archives, including those of the Pennsylvania Railroad, Westmoreland Coal, and Bethlehem Steel. Since October 1986 he has been Hagley's assistant curator of manuscripts and archives.